C000050511

Gore Vidal
History of the National Security State
&
Vidal on America

A collection of original interviews with acclaimed author Gore Vidal
conducted by Paul Jay, Senior Editor of The Real News Network
Includes a collection of original photographs

Copyright © 2014 The Real News Network

All rights reserved. No part of this book may be reproduced in any medium
without the prior written permission of The Real News Network. All photos
copyright © 2014 Paul Jay. Photos may not be copied, printed or otherwise
disseminated without the express written permission of Paul Jay.

ISBN-13: 978-1494887995
ISBN-10: 1494887991

CONTENTS

ACKNOWLEDGMENTS

Thanks to all The Real News Network volunteers who helped make this project possible.

Michael Trudeau
Alan Marwine
Sue Tinkle
Edgar Nelson
Teo Newman

FOREWORD

I met Gore Vidal in the spring of 2004 at his house in Hollywood. At the time I was organizing an international advisory committee in the early days of creating Independent World Television, which we later renamed The Real News Network.

Gore had agreed to give me twenty minutes. Two bottles of scotch and five hours later, he had told me the story of his relationship with his soul mate, Howard Austen. I asked him when we could talk about my plans for a news network. He waved his hand in his exaggerated regal fashion and said, "Who knows." He said he was off to Italy in a couple of days and if I wanted to talk further, I'd have to see him there. From the very start of The Real News I wanted Gore Vidal to be involved, so in July, I went to southern Italy.

Gore was sitting on the terrace of La Rondinaia, his cliff-top villa overlooking the Gulf of Salerno, down the coast from Naples—it's a stunning view. The red roofs of the town of Amalfi sit hundreds of feet below, with an expanse of deep sapphire sea as far as one can see. Vidal spent most of the last thirty years there in his beloved town of Ravello.

He talked about the confusion he felt since the death of his companion Howard Austen a year earlier.

"For fifty-three years I had some idea who I was, in relationship with Howard. Now, I'm not so sure."

At one point in our conversation, Gore leaned over to make a phone call, then sank back into his chair.

"I was about to call Howard."

He will soon part with the second love of his life, this Renaissance-style villa where he lived the life of an expat and hosted people like Greta Garbo, Princess Margaret, Tennessee Williams, Hillary Clinton, Sting, Mick and Bianca Jagger, and Sophia Loren.

He's done most of his writing over the last three decades in a wood-paneled study filled with books and photos.

"I run into Howard's ghost in every room. I talk to him, but he doesn't answer."

I didn't expect the raw and open way he expresses his emotions.

"I'm sufficiently Greek in attitude to be stoic, and to know that if you are too happy you will be struck down. That's what happened. I suppose I knew it was coming and was more or less prepared but you never really are. It's pretty grim living here alone, so it's time to go."

About to start his eightieth year and hobbling around on a bum knee, Vidal was not just leaving this house. He was returning to the United States, whose history and politics are his real lifelong passion.

He went back because he thought his country was in danger.

"I'm a battleship," he said. "I'm an operator. I'm a destroyer, I'm meant for war." He stopped for a long pause. "But I don't know if I can do it anymore."

For most of his life, Vidal waged a struggle against what he calls the "United States of Amnesia." Throughout a prolific career of celebrated novels, film scripts, and essays, he explored America's past, unraveled its national psyche, and railed against its misdeeds.

Most of all, it's been a fight against the hypocrisy of those who talk democracy but are more interested in the defense of property.

He comes from a ruling family (he counts Al Gore and Jackie Kennedy as kin). His father, Eugene L. Vidal, served as the first director of the Bureau of Air Commerce in the Roosevelt administration (and appeared on the cover of *Time* in 1933).

Gore knew presidents and princesses, celebrated writers and billionaires. Through his work he accumulated a significant amount of wealth and he lived very well. Yet his criticism of American society was no less compromising than that of a Chomsky or a Zinn.

He was a genuine class traitor.

Vidal could have lived an easier and more celebrated life if he just kept his mouth shut. Instead, his attacks on the American empire grew fiercer through the end of his life.

"The next national trauma will be a sharpening of class struggle. [John] Edwards got on the national ticket by noticing something that's perfectly obvious, that there are two Americas. There are those that have and those that have not. That used to be considered communist propaganda. But it is the condition in most countries most of the time, and in the United States more than ever."

We headed out to the main square of Ravello, and Gore's new knee required him to use a wheelchair for part of the trip. Settling in at his favorite bar, we watched beautiful sultry women and men circling each other in front of the cathedral of San Pantaleo.

The scene reminded me of a "Vidalism": "A narcissist is someone better looking than you are."

Streams of well-wishers, a few with raised fists in the classic anti-fascist salute, paid their respects. Gore was a hero to the European left.

We settled into more scotch. "It's a great scandal of the CEOs, who are simply bandits. They go into a company that had a rich base, grab everything they can for themselves, stock options, huge salaries, fire as many people as possible. If we ever have an old-fashioned revolution in the United States, it will be made by well-educated blue-collar workers who have lost their jobs."

Someone at our table pointed out that there didn't seem to be a sign of this—much of the working-class votes for Bush.

"Because the bandits own the media," said Gore. "And the media tells them that America is the greatest country in the world. Well, it sure as hell isn't, at least not for the people who live in it. But the media are there cheerleading, 'These are the greatest guys on earth.' The infantilizing of the republic is one of the triumphs of American television."

Gore is a man who knew media from the inside. From Hollywood, where he wrote hits like *Ben-Hur*, to a series of best-selling novels, to countless television appearances, he was one of America's great celebrity intellectuals for half a century. His transition from media darling to "extremist" outsider mirrored the process of his own radicalization. While he was much sought after around the world, there was very little room for Gore Vidal in print or on television in his own country.

When Vidal broke through as a novelist in the late forties and early fifties it was at the beginning of Cold War propaganda and McCarthyism. "The American people were now being systematically terrified by the country's ownership. I believed the whole nonsense," he writes in his memoir, *Palimpsest*. But he was starting to wake up. "My real political education began when I made money only to have it confiscated by a military machine. This confiscation of one's hard-earned money did not drive me into the right wing, as it did Ronald Reagan, who was as indignant as I but chose to blame it all on a vague nemesis called 'big government.' I started to turn left. If the government was going to take so much of our money, then let the government give us health care, education, and all those other things first-world countries provide their taxpayers."

By the sixties, Vidal's fame as a writer and a political pundit had grown. He supported Kennedy at the 1960 Democratic convention and was a frequent visitor at the White House after that. His social critique had sharpened. In 1960, the *New York Sunday News* under the headline "The Legend and the Wrecker" captions a photo of JFK and Gore as "A playwright-novelist sets out to defame anything and everything in U.S. politics."

Jackie Kennedy was his stepsister, and he spent time getting to know Jack. "We were both unadventurous conservatives, interested in personal glory . . . the only division between us would have been my growing hatred of the empire and his unquestioning love for it. In due course, he wanted us to win the cold war with a hot war. I think, even then, I suspected that the cold war was a fraud." Still, Vidal bought into the Kennedy myth: "What an actor he was! What a gullible audience I was!"

Vidal's critique of American society grew more profound during the sixties. He joined the antiwar movement's opposition to the U.S. invasion of Vietnam. His wit and celebrity gave him a platform few with his views could command. His 1968 debate with William F. Buckley Jr., on ABC's live televised coverage of the Democratic convention, is legendary. In it he calls Buckley a "crypto-Nazi," and Buckley threatens to "sock" him in the face.

His stardom continued to rise. In 1969, the release of the movie based on his novel *Myra Breckinridge* made the cover of *Time* magazine. The publishing of his novel *1876* was the occasion for Vidal himself to join his father on a *Time* cover in 1976 (one of the few things he shares with the Bush family). When Gore spoke, the media listened.

By the nineties, after exploring American history in a series of novels, the picture became clearer for Vidal. He writes that the key turning point was after World War II. Instead of demobilizing the army, Truman expanded the war machine and ushered in the National Security State. Kennedy raised military spending $17 billion above that of the Eisenhower years.

Writing in 1994: "I realize how little understanding any of us had of what was actually going on at the time. We had been carefully conditioned to believe that the gallant, lonely USA was, on every side, beleaguered by the Soviet Union, a monolithic Omnipotency; we now know that they were weak and reactive while we were strong and provocative. Once Jack had inherited the make-believe war against communism in general and the Soviet Union in particular, he preceded, unknown to all but a few, to change the rules of the game. He was about to turn Truman's pseudo-war into a real war."

With that realization, the two pillars of the American postwar narrative fell: the Cold War and Kennedy mythologies shattered. Vidal broke the limits of what American media, particularly television, finds as acceptable criticism. He was no longer considered "loyal opposition."

His writing on Timothy McVeigh in *Vanity Fair* in 1998 explored the American patriot movement, insisting we couldn't write Oklahoma bomber McVeigh off as an evil madman. Instead we should try to understand the alienation of rural families dispossessed by big government and agribusiness. He was denounced in a *Salon* article as having "gone postal" and having joined the "black helicopter crowd."

After 9/11, he was more isolated by U.S. media. *Vanity Fair*, long a favored home for Vidal's renowned essays, refused to print his piece written in the weeks following the events. It was later published in an Italian book, whose title translates into English as "The end of liberty: Toward a new totalitarianism," and later in the *Guardian* newspaper. The piece finally made it to the U.S. in Vidal's book of essays titled *Perpetual War for*

Perpetual Peace: How We Got to Be So Hated. The book became a "surprise" best seller.

In this book and in his *Dreaming War: Blood for Oil and the Cheney-Bush Junta* and *Imperial America*, Vidal elaborates his critique of the national security state and asserts that fifty years of imperial U.S. foreign policy contributed to the events of 9/11.

He sifts through the information surrounding the attacks and suggests that the Bush administration might have knowingly allowed the terrorist attacks to take place to gain political advantage, both domestically and internationally (writing before the war in Iraq, he suggests one motive is to overthrow the Taliban in order to create the conditions for the building of a U.S.-controlled oil pipeline). He also called for an investigation of the Saudi and Pakistani role in the creation of al-Qaeda and the deadly trail of attacks that followed.

For suggesting that the Bush administration might have been deliberately inactive in preventing the attacks, he was battered from many quarters. He wasn't saying much not said by others, but this was Gore Vidal, a man who could command attention. He was of course denounced as a conspiracy theorist, compared to the creators of the *Protocols of Zion*.

He had been accused of saying Bush organized a grand conspiracy to bring about the attacks, and he says that this is lunacy. "I've never said that," Gore insisted several times. In going over his work, I found that he's never made the argument. He clearly believed the White House might have been able to prevent the attacks if they wanted to, and that they didn't want to.

Since he published these books, we know the White House did in fact use the 9/11 events as a false pretext for the Iraq War.

We also know from the 9/11 Commission that the Bush administration did know an attack was coming. We also know they did nothing about it. *Why* is still a matter of debate, but surely the questions Vidal and others raise must be considered. Incompetency on the scale suggested by the commission is possible, but hard to comprehend. Vidal says, if it is such, why have heads not rolled?

This debate has been more or less closed down in the monopoly media (interestingly enough, many 9/11 family members are asking the same questions as Vidal, and refuse to accept official explanations).

The next day, I returned to the villa. Gore was reading a newspaper, leaning back on a large couch so wide it makes it impossible to sit up straight.

As Gore readied to join the battle in the U.S., he was uncertain of his reception and doubtful of his abilities. And Howard was not in his corner.

So why go? How important is the 2004 election?

"Bush is a fool, and he is putting us all in danger."

Is Kerry much better?

"No, but I don't see him rushing around doing preemptive strikes against countries that displease him."

In terms of the threat of dictatorship you talk about, is the danger less with Kerry?

"You can't tell. You can't tell what tactic he might use to frighten the people in order to get legislation that he wants in Congress. Frightening the people is the greatest weapon of American would-be dictators. So you don't know what box he'll get himself into. I think he's probably too shrewd to get into something as stupid as Bush has done."

After the barrage of criticism he came under the last couple of years, and the emotional loss of his partner, I wondered if he was ready to stick his neck out again.

"If Bush is elected again there will be another war. I feel particularly committed to sticking my neck out this time because it's going to be my neck along with everybody else in the country."

I asked him again why he's doing it. Why not enjoy his retirement and write the follow-up to his memoirs? The twinkle in his eye fired up, and he sat upright with a resolute defiance. "Because I love a fight." It's a great burst of energy; he is "the destroyer."

I often met with Gore upon his return to the United States. We spent many evenings together, consuming more scotch. We finally got to talk about The Real News Network and he became a vocal supporter of our work.

These days the media is more interested in Gore's estate and sex life than his political opinions. I don't know anything about that part of his life. A few times he spoke about sexuality being a spectrum, but it wasn't a subject we spent any time on. We talked about history and the politics of empire.

We sat down for several long interview sessions between 2005 and 2007 and this book is a collection of the best of that material.

Gore died on July 31, 2012, at the age of eighty-six.

Paul Jay

PAUL JAY VISITING GORE VIDAL
SUMMER OF 2004

The Cold War

JAY: Was the bombing of Hiroshima and Nagasaki the closing curtain of World War II or the opening act of the Cold War?

VIDAL: Probably the opening act of the Cold War; it was also the end of the American Republic. Every single important military commander on the American side pleaded with the new president. Our great Augustus, Franklin Roosevelt, had died, in I think it was April of forty-five, and was succeeded by a no-brainer called Harry Truman, who didn't know what he was doing.

But he had learned certain notes. He'd been vice president for a few weeks only. Roosevelt had never told him about the atomic bomb. So he arrives as president, and advisers, all the people connected with the bombs, wanted to drop them so they'd spent their money well. Truman thought it was a good idea because he thought that we needed an enemy. We'd had Hitler and Nazism. Stalin and communism—even better.

And while he was at Potsdam with his first meeting with Stalin, he gets news from Alamogordo, New Mexico, that the atom bomb works. He's overexcited 'cause he's going to give it to Stalin, 'cause he was a good American who never really read a book, except for some very simple children's stories about American history. So he thought, looking at Stalin, "Here's the enemy, just made for us. We can militarize the economy; we can increase the army." Then word comes: The bomb works, as reported by Leslie Groves, who was a student, at West Point, of my father. And Groves—very pompous fellow, and quite full of himself. It was [J. Robert] Oppenheimer who should have been filled with himself, because Oppenheimer really gave us the bomb—with great misgivings.

When the explosion went off in the New Mexican desert, he was almost in tears. This is Dr. Oppenheimer. And he said, "Lo, behold, I am Shiva, the destroyer of worlds." Then the decision was made—there was a very good book by a man called Gar Alperovitz on the decision to use the bomb. At least Truman had the good sense to consult his military camp commanders. Every last one of them, including the man Curtis Lemay—Dr. Strangelove, General Strangelove—said, "Don't do it."

Eisenhower in Europe, the commanding general there, Nimitz, the commanding admiral in the Pacific, they said, "Don't you do it. We'll be hated by the whole world. Japan is defeated. Everybody knows it. The emperor has been writing Truman letters, asking for surrender." Truman, much like the current president [George W. Bush], he didn't know anything about foreign affairs, but he knew he had two weapons, he had two aces in the hole, or however they say it in poker, and he's going to play them.

And he played them. And the cost to our reputation. I mean, the meditations of Eisenhower on how horrible this would be for the United States! I think he suspected he'd already be an American president by then, and there was going to be nothing but trouble. And there's been nothing but trouble for us ever since. Truman went on with this grotesque adventure, and we have gone on in the wake of it, and the Cold War begins.

The Emperor

JAY: One of the principles of U.S. foreign policy coming out of World War II was to establish a single-superpower world. Was one of the reasons for the dropping of the nuclear weapons to tell the world—a shot across the bow, if you will—that this is going to be a single-superpower world?

VIDAL: I don't think it was that well thought out. We had single-handedly won World War II. The Russians don't agree with this because without their land armies we would never have liberated Europe from the Nazis. So the Russians paid a great cost in life and treasure, as they like to say. And they won the ground war, we won the air war, and we won the sea war. And that was about it. But we grabbed all the credit for everything, as we are wont to do.

Europeans have always noticed we'd come in very, very late into their European wars. And if they followed the advice of people like me, we would never have come in to go at war abroad as we did in World War I, as we did again in World War II. But we lacked by forty-five—when the bombs were dropped or considered—we lacked Franklin Roosevelt. He was the emperor. He knew exactly what he was doing.

He made a number of agreements with Stalin at Yalta. All Stalin asked for was to be treated as a normal superpower, which is what they were. Roosevelt did not have any nonsense going on in his head about the sanctity of Christianity, the sanctity of capitalism versus communism. I don't think he ever gave such topics a thought. All he knew is we had won the war, and he was going to decolonialize.

Now, that is the great Roosevelt message. He told Churchill at Yalta, he said, you know, "Now we're winning, you know, the war in Europe." Pacific war was still going on. "But now that we're winning it, you know that you're going to have to give up India." "Oh, yes, of course, we always knew that. And one day we'll really give it up." And he said, "No, no, no, you're going to give it up right away. And France is going to give up Indochina. Sumatra and Java are going to be let go free by the Dutch." And he said, "I don't care what this does to European powers. I'm ending colonialism, because without a clean sweep, United States is meaningless."

I mean, Roosevelt was a great statesman, and he knew a lot about geography, and these other jokers didn't know it. And so it came to pass that Churchill had to give up India, grumbling all the way. At this famous lunch, a lot of witnesses there, Churchill apparently turned to him. He thought this man was his friend, but emperors have no friends. And he said, "What do you want me to do? Get on my hind legs like your little dog Fala, and beg?" The emperor said, "Yes." You don't take on emperors in their own empire.

Roosevelt had done what he set out to do. Why did he set out to do what he did? He had lived through World War I, and he'd come to Washington as assistant secretary of the navy, under Woodrow Wilson, one of the wooliest-headed presidents we ever had. I mean, he makes Harry Truman look like Einstein. He tries out the League of Nations, which he didn't know how to set it up. He antagonized half the Senate and then wondered why they voted against him. Roosevelt had learned his lesson from Woodrow Wilson.

So he sets up the United Nations. Wisely, he put Eleanor Roosevelt, who was in many ways a better statesman than he, in charge of just seeing that it got off to a good start, because he suspected he was dying and indeed did die. And she nursed it along. And it was a very good thing until American right wingers got a hold of it, 'cause they had to complain about foreigners. You know, foreigners are bad people. They don't wash, and they never pay back their debts.

JAY: Roosevelt was planning his vision of the American Empire?

VIDAL: Of course he was. One of the first things he did was tell Churchill, "Goodbye, India. You're out of the empire business. There are no empires." He didn't say we're going to be the only one, because he was too tactful and too manipulative. Somebody might have said, no you're not. But he set everything up in the postwar world.

JAY: He makes the deal with Ibn Saud on a boat off Great Bitter Lake.

VIDAL: Yeah, on his way back from Yalta on a battleship. And Ibn Saud, the king of Saudi Arabia, came aboard and spent the entire day. And here's Roosevelt, a dying man, saying, you know, "I'm rather looking forward to coming here after the war. I can help you with many things." He was going to help him with the price of oil, I suppose. And Roosevelt was still very vigorous; it's just his flesh gave out. And so he came to die at Warm Springs, Georgia. On a sad day.

JAY: That deal with Ibn Saud seemed to set the pattern for the next fifty, sixty years of Middle East regional policy.

VIDAL: Well, and the conflict with the Brits, because the Brits were in Iranian oil. Amoco, whatever company British Oil, Petroleum. And the Brits could think of nothing else. And Roosevelt thought, *Well, I'll preempt that sooner or later with the American alliance with the Arabians.* And they quite liked each other, the two old kings. And they sat there and divided up that sphere of influence. Then Roosevelt was dead, and Ibn Saud was never a great player, and so that was the end of that.

JAY: But it did set some of the pattern, this use of Wahhabism and the Saudi royal family in the Middle East politics.

VIDAL: Well, I don't think Roosevelt knew anything about the Wahhabi Muslims. He didn't do a lot of research. But he had great instincts. He knew where the oil was, and he knew where the power was, so he accommodated the power of the royal family there, and he smiled benignly at the oil wells.

On Liberty

We've always been an oligarchy of the well-to-do and are becoming even more so now. What freedoms we had have now been eliminated—Magna Carta guaranteed us due process of law, the only good thing England left us. —Gore Vidal

JAY: In this period after World War II and this sort of feeling of world supremacy, domestically we see McCarthyism.

VIDAL: Well, McCarthy kind of misread the tarot cards. You know, he thought it was a simple matter of conquest. Probably the only thing he basically cared about was Ireland, because he was an Irishman. And he liked the British Empire being kicked in the butt by Americans. So anything that would, you know, do them in or do in, you know, Dean Acheson, the secretary of state, who seemed like an Englishman. I think he did a lot of, you know, ethnic one-upmanship.

But no. Well, first of all, we were taken over by big business, as we always have been, but this time it was pretty severe because the stakes were greater. Somebody said—oh, the kid last night who was interviewing me, Adam something—he said, you know, "Certainly the United States is basically an altruistic country. Look at the Marshall Plan." I said, "What's altruistic about seizing control of Western Europe? It seems to be very much part of an imperial plan." Oh, he couldn't believe it. He just thought we did it out of goodness of heart.

Now, he's a very bright guy, writes for the *New Yorker* and so on, yet he's been so misled. And he reads a lot of history; he's very intelligent. You cannot get through the density of the propaganda with which the American people, through the dreaded media, have been filled and the horrible public educational system we have for the average person. It's just grotesque.

JAY: There's this fundamental belief, religious belief, that America's foreign policy since World War II has been a fight for freedom.

VIDAL: Well, it never was. And the belief that we're a democracy. That means you know nothing about the Constitution. The people who made the Constitution hated democracy. Some of them put up with it better than others. Jefferson was pretty good on the subject. The others just loathed it.

JAY: But certainly there's more democracy in the United States than there was in Hitler's Germany?

VIDAL: Well, I suppose that if you're being tortured to death by Mao Tse-tung, it's much better to be with Paul Revere in front of a fireplace in Concord, New Hampshire.

JAY: But there are stages of this process of democracy or lack thereof.

VIDAL: The *Federalist Papers* are very clear. Whenever

one of the founding fathers and one of the people who was inventing the Constitution, they start to get apoplectic at the mention of Athens, the mention of Pericles, the mention of democracy. They go on and on about mobs, and we don't want this, and we don't want that. We're an oligarchy of the well-to-do. We were at the very beginning, when the Constitution was made, and we're even more so now.

JAY: But within that context there is more or less the right of free assembly. There is more or less the right of free speech. Of course, you have more free speech if you own a television network than if you don't.

VIDAL: Well, yes, as you'll find out with The Real News.

JAY: But there are some constitutional rights here that you wouldn't have seen—

VIDAL: They've been eliminated one by one over the last four years.

JAY: That's my question.

VIDAL: When habeas corpus was removed, I think they attributed it to certain desires of the USA Patriot Act. When they got rid of that, they got rid of Magna Carta. When you get rid of that, you get rid of our liberties. This, the only good thing England ever left us was Magna Carta.

Magna Carta guarantees due process of law. You cannot have your life removed, you cannot have your money removed, your freedom removed, except by a trial by jury of your peers, and you could be represented by legal counsel—that's been eliminated. Sixth Amendment is gone. The speed with which it was done is sort of miraculous, because this is a screw-up administration—they can't do anything properly.

There are those who keep quoting me, because I had said, well, they'd had enough warnings about 9/11 to have done something. Well, that's the CIA's warning. They did nothing. So I have to face this every now and then. "Well, you said that Bush was in favor of it. Can you prove that?" I said, "Of course I can't. How would I know?" I do know that he is so incompetent—this was a great, successful mission conducted by some crazed religious zealots.

U.S. Media and Society

The people have no voice because they have no information. —Gore Vidal

JAY: There's a lot of taboo subjects in the media, and even sometimes in the society.

VIDAL: Particularly in the society.

JAY: Yeah. But one of them is trying to draw any historical lessons from the rise of fascism in Germany, in Italy, and say there's anything in common—

VIDAL: I'm not joking when I refer to our country as the United States of Amnesia, although I was corrected recently by Studs Terkel out of Chicago. And he said, "Gore, it's not the United States of Amnesia; it's the United States of Alzheimer's." I stand corrected.

JAY: Fascism in Germany wasn't a coup; it was a many-year process. I'm not suggesting we're living in an equivalent period, but there are lessons to be learned.

VIDAL: But it is equivalent. I mean, don't be shy of saying that. The response to the Reichstag fire is precisely that to 9/11, which was invoked by this administration's people. "And if we don't fight them over there, we got to fight 'em here." This little fool. How are they going to get here? Greyhound bus? I mean, he is so stupid himself that he assumes everybody else is equally stupid. If he had been really elected, I would say everybody else was stupid, but he wasn't.

JAY: But the party that was really elected went along with most of what he did until very recently.

VIDAL: Oh, he didn't do much of anything. They went along applauding it because they were getting huge contracts for Halliburton.

JAY: No, I'm talking about the leadership of the Democratic Party went along with the Patriot Act, went along with the war in Iraq.

VIDAL: Have you ever found them? You know where they live?

JAY: The leadership of the Democratic Party?

VIDAL: You know, they're not visible. There's some obviously good people in the party. I like Dennis Kucinich, I like Senator Leahy. There are some very good people in Congress. And let's hope they start doing some oversight. But I'm not very sanguine.

JAY: In the period between 9/11 and Katrina, where in Katrina some cracks started to appear in the Bush armor, we saw a kind of capitulation by American media and all the opposition political leadership. And you saw a face of America that we might see more of.

VIDAL: After all, you are in opposition to American media, and so am I. And we know how false it is, and how corrupt it is, and how eager they are for mischief, making money for the ownership of the country. There's nothing to be done about them. And no wonder, even when the American people might ever again, which I doubt, have an uncorrupted presidential election—2000 was corrupted, 2004 was corrupted.

I don't think we'll ever get to know the people's voice, and the people have no voice because they have no information. That is why you're doing useful work here. That's why I'm chatting with you here. That could be useful, to tell them actually what happens around the world.

That poor guy running for Congress, everybody jumped on him, particularly angry people. He suggested that our foreign policy might have had something to do with 9/11, that we were deeply disliked in the Muslim world for other reasons. It's the same presidential, I guess. "Do you believe in evolution?" said this idiot. I mean, to reveal the leadership of the United States hasn't made it to the twentieth century, that our leadership is as ignorant as that. Five of them said, no, no, thinking little lord Jesus was going to vote for them.

JAY: It's in these moments of crisis, like terrorist attacks, that you start to see people's colors.

VIDAL: Yellow.

JAY: In Britain as well, I was really taken aback. After the London bus bombings, Ken Livingstone—"Red Ken" Livingstone—was asked, was there any connection between these bombings and U.K. foreign policy, and he said there's no connection whatsoever. This is just people that hate our way of life.

VIDAL: Yeah, that's the new lie that they like to tell. Well, that's Bush all the time. They just hate us. Why? Nobody has to ask them why. He doesn't know why. "Well, they envy us, our form of government." Who envies us? That can of worms we've got in Washington? And it's been many years in the United States since I have seen a Norwegian coming to get a green card.

Democrats and Religion

The Democratic Party is a machine to get votes for its people. None of whom should probably be elected to the high offices of state. The Republican Party is fundamentally crooked. —Gore Vidal

JAY: This idea that this un-democratization or growth of fascism is incremental—what are the other signs of it in American society?

VIDAL: Well, it's been the monopolizing of great wealth, which tends to happen in basically unjust societies and undemocratic societies. We have plenty of would-be democrats and would-be liberals, would-be progressives. But how do you organize?

The Democratic Party is a machine to get votes for its people, none of whom should probably be elected to the high offices of state. That's all. The Republican Party is fundamentally crooked and might well be outlawed one of these days. Le Pen, you know, in France, who is an out-and-out fascist, the French have managed in some clever way to contain him.

I mean, he's always running for president, and his votes never seem to show up. I don't know how they do it, but we've got to do that with the Republican base, the religious right. We don't want them running the country. Nobody does. Certainly not the founding fathers. And I think we have to ride herd on them and make sure they do not seize the state.

JAY: Well, they kind of did, and—

VIDAL: Of course they did. They took advantage of 9/11 and so on.

JAY: How do you assess this danger to democracy of the organization of the hard right alliance of evangelicals?

VIDAL: Well, you have to work out what it is. They are a little splinter. They can't summon many voters at any given time. They are a minority of a minority of a minority. They have everybody buffaloed because the great corporations like them and pay money to their candidates for sheriff and senator. And they're playing big-time politics. Yes, indeed.

But the average person doesn't like them. You know, any time I want to get applause—and I lecture across America in state after state after state—when I fear things are getting a little low, I always say, "And another thing: let us tax all the religions." I bring down the goddamn house with that. And any politician would if he had sense enough to do it. The people don't like their tax exemption.

JAY: I went to a church in Nashville, evangelical church. I was there for a four and a half hour service. And in four and a half hours the words *poor* or *poverty* did not cross anyone's lips.

VIDAL: No. They might have fallen off the lips.

JAY: My understanding of Christianity is the fundamental criteria you'll be judged by to enter salvation, is your attitude to the poor, which doesn't get talked about much. But there was an interesting thing. I met a man there who's married to a friend who has quite progressive politics, but he's a believer and goes to the church. And he said 20, 25 percent of the church does not support the right wing politics and didn't vote for Bush.

VIDAL: I'm sure of that.

JAY: There's an interesting fracture in terms of the honest people who believe in the values espoused and what's getting expressed at the political level.

VIDAL: Well, remember, all that area from which the Gore family comes was solid Democrat and progressive under Roosevelt for several decades. So they just didn't become Republicans because they all wanted to be bankers; they became it because they didn't like black people, and they thought the Democrats were pushing integration too fast. And that's how the great split came about, to the shame of the whole country.

The Future

We've got to get back the pillars of the Constitution.

I was born eighty years ago in a country called the United States of America and now I live in a Homeland—an expression we haven't heard since Hitler. —Gore Vidal

JAY: How significantly different would a Clinton White House, Obama White House, or an Edwards White House—how much can they do? How much do they want to do differently?

VIDAL: It's too broken. The first thing you have to do is get back habeas corpus. You've got to get back the Magna Carta, you've got to get back our legal system, you've got to get back the pillars of the Constitution, and they're gone. Republics don't restore themselves.

JAY: There's a group of ex-Reagan conservatives that are waging a campaign exactly along these lines, saying the Constitution must be reclaimed. In fact, they're making more of it than the leadership of the Democratic Party is.

VIDAL: Well, do they have the same constitution in mind? Or do they have something else in mind? One never knows with marginal groups. I think the Reagan people just believed in "You make as much money as you can, screw everybody else."

JAY: This gang seems to be, they're certainly talking the talk of wanting to defend habeas corpus and the

Constitution. But more my point is, we're hearing very little of this from the Democratic Party.

VIDAL: Well, people know that there's Dennis Kucinich. There are a lot of people, Senator Leahy, Congressman Conyers—there are a lot of people who understand the Constitution and understand the risks of dictatorship, because we're right on the edge of it. I tell people, Europeans that say, you know, "What do you think of the regime?" I said, "Well, what they've done is interesting. Symbolic." I said, "I was born eighty years ago in a country called the United States of America, and I now live in a homeland."

It's an expression we haven't heard since Hitler. Since they don't know anything about language or politics or thought or anything else, they think this is a wonderful way of explaining the United States defending itself against its numerous inscrutable enemies. They hate us. We don't know why. Well, if we didn't blow up their cities, they might feel more kindly towards us. Two plus two is not possible in the United States of Alzheimer's.

JAY: What do you see in the next ten, fifteen years?

VIDAL: Bankruptcy for the nation, which will put an end to these insane wars. We can't afford one. I know in Washington, I mean, the entire Bush gang is longing to reconstitute the army with another million men, and it can't find a million men. And the American people, although they can be easily tricked, they're not stupid, and they're not enlisting.

JAY: Those who've been more or less running the world for the last fifty, sixty years or more, how do they deal with the situation where they might not run the world anymore?

VIDAL: Well, martial law would be the first step that they would take to get back their powers. It's always a good one, always an easy one. They have all sorts of models, they think, in Abraham Lincoln, but he certainly ruled with dictatorial powers, but the Constitution allowed him to do that, and he was faced with the dissolution of his country, which he cared a lot about.

There's nobody in this administration who knows anything about the United States. They don't know the history. They certainly do not wish the people well. If you ever talk to Republicans privately about that—this is elected officials—their opinion of the people, their contempt is so total. And if you're on their side, you're a softhearted liberal or you've been taken in.

JAY: What do you see as the response coming from the people in the next ten, fifteen years?

VIDAL: Well, I think, bankruptcy, depression.

JAY: How will people respond?

VIDAL: Well, there could be rioting. Certainly when we saw what happened in the late twenties, early thirties, institutions collapsed, banks collapsed, and Roosevelt's swift actions followed by the brains of Lord Keynes changed the whole economic structure of the West, much less the United States. So we were lucky between Keynes and Roosevelt to have had two such extraordinary men who did have our interests at heart or at least appeared to.

The State of Media and The Real News

Everybody with an IQ above room temperature is onto the con act of our media. They are obeying bigger, richer interests than informing the public—which is the last thing that corporate America has ever been interested in doing. —Gore Vidal

JAY: The economic structure of television makes what I'm going to ask difficult to accomplish. But do you think television journalists have learned anything from this last four years?

VIDAL: Well, they've always been lazy, and they're not used to getting to the heart of problems, of matters. They're not used to investigating anything. Socrates tells us that the unexamined life is not worth living, and that is an absolute truth. Those who want to examine life don't go in for journalism, because they're not allowed to. So they've got to be very careful. They have to think about tenure if they're at a university. They've got to think about, you know, the publisher and advertisers. So it's a difficult row to hoe, and we have no intellectual tradition of any kind in the United States. I even told Arthur Schlesinger, "You know, Arthur, one Schlesinger does not make a spring." He was horrified.

JAY: What do you think is the significance of what we're trying to do?

VIDAL: Well, I'm all for it. I wouldn't be sitting here today if I didn't like the notion. And it's apt to catch on.

It's when the news starts to break, how two presidential elections, 2000 and 2004, were stolen and the *New York Times* would not review the book written about it by Congressman Conyers, nor *Washington Post*, nor *Wall Street Journal*, the great instruments of news were silent.

Well, they're saying, we don't give a goddamn about the United States. Just stew in your own juice. Leave us alone. We have corporate figures to add up now, and we have certain things we want to put in place, and we may have a couple of candidates for you dum-dums, but you probably won't like them.

You know, I've been around the ruling class all my life, and I've been quite aware of their total contempt for the people of the country. And the Republican machine became so good at transmitting its own feelings about the world to the enemy, to the liberals, once anyone, any of the right wing hear what I just said, he'll say, "Oh, the liberals have always hated America. We know that. They despise family values, because they're only interested in gang bangs and drugs and so forth." This is the way they deal.

And whenever they have a real coward for president, like Bush himself, and you have a hero like Kerry, "Oh, he's a coward. Didn't you know that? We've got five guys who were in Vietnam with him." What they do is whatever is their transgression, whatever are their faults, they lie and apply it to the other person. That confuses everything.

If I were an average voter in the United States, I wouldn't know who was telling the truth, whether Kerry really had run away and didn't get Purple Hearts, or whether Junior, you know, had actually learned how to fly a plane.

JAY: And television news covers the lies like news.

VIDAL: Yes. It has a lock on it.

JAY: You've been touring the country after your new book.

VIDAL: Well, no, I was touring it before the last congressional election to raise money for the Democratic Party. Not that I like the Democratic Party, but we have to have the semblance of a second party to get rid of these others.

JAY: What do you hear from people?

VIDAL: Well, I've never heard cries of rage so loud. It's when I'm in New Mexico or West Virginia. I've covered the whole country by now.

JAY: Our project's fundamentally motivated out of our own concern for what the future holds, especially in terms of what democratic rights we do have and the way the media has played such a destructive role. What do you think is the potential for what we're doing? What do you make of the project?

47

VIDAL: Well, the potential is enormous. There's not anyone with an IQ above, you know, lowest room temperature who isn't interested in something like this. Everybody is onto the con act of our media, that they are obeying bigger, richer interests than informing the public, which is the last thing that corporate America has ever been interested in doing.

So I think, you know, the sky's the limit to the amount of audience you can get. And one of the secrets is, aside from telling the truth, which most people in America hate because they've been brought up on advertising, and they think the truth is just something irrelevant, you know. "Everybody lies."

You know, I love that line. So it's all right to steal the election. Well, that isn't what the world's about. And I think it's really come down to we're going to be blown up one of these days. We have now acquired so many enemies with so much power in the world that, well, they're going to take a couple of cracks at us.

I would rather have The Real News here telling us just where it was they struck, where it is intelligence says they may strike again, and maybe why they're doing it. We blew up their mosque, we killed their president, or whatever it was that set them off. What our fictional news does now and this is all it is fiction, whether it's CNN or CBS or NBC, it's all fiction. The people making this junk know that. The viewers suspect it. But where are they going to turn to? Where are they going to find out?

They can't all go out and get a, you know, subscription to the *Nation*, which would help straighten them out, at least in print. So you're going to be the only alternative, and the word will start to spread. Look at the speed with which, you know, just by telling jokes, John Stewart and company, got the attention of everybody. And now they say, well, most of the real news that the people know about they get from the satirizing of it that Stewart does. And very funny he is, too. In other words you build a better mousetrap, and the mouse will come to your door.

The History of the National Security State

JAY: When last we talked was before the [2004] election, and you were getting ready to come back to participate in the fight. How do you assess America after the reelection, legally at least, or in some form of *legally* of President Bush?

VIDAL: Well, as I was preparing to come back for the election, I did predict that in 2000 the election was well and truly stolen, absolutely, in front of the nation, later in front of the Supreme Court, which was the decisive selector of the election. And as we were coming up to 2004, I made a prediction that Bush would lose again, but he would serve a second term because they'd had four years to steal this election.

They learn. I mean, these are assiduous people. If they could get away with the mess that they had in Florida, the lady with the mascara—Ms. Harris, you know—and I mean, there was every overt trick that you could play. I said, "Think of how much they've learned in the four years since 2000." Well, they did.

We've just seen the Conyers report out of Ohio. They did all the same tricks: They got the secretary of state of Ohio in charge of elections, as Ms. Harris, secretary of state of Florida, was in charge of. Both Ms. Harris and the secretary of state of Ohio were co-chairs of the Bush-Cheney election—reelection committees, which strikes me as a little much, but they did it again. But it was much more expert. They had many, many more electronic—without paper trail—it was just smoothly done.

Our ever-corrupt media—which is now being, at last, cracked open by what we're doing, I trust—the ever-corrupt media decided nobody likes a sore loser. Well, we lost the republic. I don't care about Gore or Kerry, but I do care about the republic and about our votes being recorded. Our votes were not recorded. There were stacks of them sitting around Florida in back rooms. They talked about the recount; well, they never got around to the *count*. So they could say in all honesty, well, you know, the recount was almost done and so forth. Yeah, but the count wasn't done.

The same thing happened in Ohio. Congressman Conyers, one of the few really useful people in Congress, Michigan Democrat, minority head of the judiciary committee, went out there with a bunch of other congressmen and some loyal staffers, and they went from every district, every county in Ohio to see what happened. They talked. The secretary of state would not answer any questions. Now, he was in charge of the corruption. There's a vast case to be made against him.

JAY: What are some of the examples of how they did this?

VIDAL: Well, there was just—there are so many. There was one which made me laugh but must have made others weep. Nine thousand voters reported for duty to vote. And, you know, they had to line up a bit. They were—they weren't kept waiting too long. And then they went through and they cast their—pressed that electronic voting machine. Triad, not Diebold this time, was a principal culprit. And afterwards they—

JAY: These are the voting machines?

VIDAL: Yeah, the voting machines. And Triad makes voting machines. And Triad had issued to the various people who were handling the ballots with a cheat sheet—how many votes we're going to need for governor, how many votes for the sheriff, how many— to make it look legitimate. So they were aiming at a certain number of votes per office. But this one balloting place just went crazy. I mean, too much pressure had been put on these people. So it ended up with nine thousand people—we know that; that was recorded—they came in to vote.

By some extraordinary act of grace (I believe religious people call it), some act of grace, not one of the nine thousand cast a vote for president. They were just too busy with alderman, with sheriff, with school board. Another case in which—after all, Kerry was the best-financed Democratic presidential candidate in many years, if ever. And yet, in another congressional— another district in Ohio, he got almost no votes at all, whereas two unknown, third-party people split a huge slice of votes, which had been transferred over to them. So never rule out the nervousness of the hands of thieves. Their hands were shaking, and sometimes, you know, the surveyor got all the votes.

JAY: Now, you would think fraud in a presidential election should be one of the great news stories of anyone's career as a journalist. This hasn't even broken the ice of the television news and, barely, print.

VIDAL: Well, barely print—I can testify to that, because when Conyers got back from Ohio, a small Chicago firm, publishers, published a book of his findings, and there's—everything is very carefully done and legally done, and he had some good staffers with him. We know almost everything about what was done in that election, and practically nothing was honest.

Where is the newspaper of record, the *New York Times*? God, how we used to swear by this. I mean, it just shines in the night with nobility, the *New York Times*, and probity too. Not one word of the Conyers report has appeared in the *New York Times*. And I even read Section F, you know, I even go through the real estate section to see if it's been hidden away there, because they like to say, "Well, we printed it. You just didn't see that Sunday."

No, it's Saturday—Saturday is the day that they print the news that they don't want you to read, because they know that's the one paper nobody looks at. Not one word about the Conyers report, the most distinguished man of the judiciary committee. And he spent a lot of time and effort.

JAY: There was a critical moment, I guess, the day of the election, the night of the results, where it was already suspect of Ohio, and Kerry had to decide whether or not he was going to raise the objection or concede. He chose, for his own reasons, to concede, which is a story, but the media conceded with him. It clearly should have been a major story, whether or not Kerry decided to pursue it. But doesn't that tell us something about the way the media seems to cover everything? That if it isn't within the limits of the way the debate's being framed by those close to or in power, there's no independent journalism?

VIDAL: No, there is no independent journalism in the interconnection between the forces of darkness and the media itself—in arms, sometimes, the forces of darkness. But the head of Diebold, which is one of the makers of electronic balloting machinery, wrote a notorious letter about a year ago to the Republican voters of Ohio: "Boy, we're going to deliver this state for Bush." And he sure did.

His machines were doing it, anyway. These are conflicts of interest, which, you know, smack of notoriousness. A real press would bring it up. How it is basically done, I don't know, except too few people own too many outlets—newspaper owners own TV stations, TV stations own publishers, and so it goes.

And so our republic went. Two presidential elections in a row, where the people's will has not been expressed, and where you begin to think—I mean, paranoia does start to blossom in all this—when Kerry starts to make some of the gaffes before the end, well, you begin to wonder, well, what team is he on?

When he came out and said, "Well, all right. Had I known what we know now, that there were no weapons of mass destruction, I still would have been for the war," well, at that moment, you just come and take him away. He didn't know why he was running.

JAY: It's a little late to prove you're not a flip-flopper, not quite the right moment.

VIDAL: Well, he flopped, if not flipped. And that's been the case all along, that these extraordinary likenesses. I thought Gore would put up a better fight, since it is in our genetic heritage to battle these things. He seemed so overwhelmed at being thought a sore loser. Well, if you've lost the presidency when you've already gained the popular vote by several hundred thousand votes, and the Electoral College, as everybody knows, an easily manipulated bad joke at our expense, a present from our founding fathers to make sure that we never have democracy, that the people will never rule. And that's why the Electoral College was invented, that's why they retain it: It's too convenient.

JAY: It seems that in both elections the Democratic Party leadership were terrified of letting the Constitutional Crisis Genie out of the bottle, and more scared than the Republicans seemed to be.

VIDAL: Well, the Republicans feared nothing, since they had all the machinery in place, and the old ladies in Florida were kept out in two-hundred-degree sunlight so that they would be fainting by the time they got to the polling booth. People of a dusky hue were certainly not allowed to vote very often, because they were suspected of being felons. Nobody quite knew why, but they were felons.

So, I mean, the vote was denied millions of people all across the country, but particularly the suspect areas like Florida and, this time, Ohio. You know, Ohio is the heartland of the United States. It's the old Western Reserve, where the New Englanders went when they went west. Well, first stop was Ohio. Mother of Presidents, it was known. It's a serious state. It's a state with everything in it. It's got—you know, so a lot of Rust Belt, but it's got a lot of progressives. It's kind of a model state. But if you've got the secretary of state, who determines the weight of the paper with which you make your application to vote to be put on the rolls—he came up with this incredible weight of the paper. If it was not done on a certain kind of paper— and who goes around weighing paper, for God's sake? You'd just go and get a piece of paper. He said, "Oh, it had to be bond paper, two-point-seven, or otherwise it is not a ballot."

JAY: But how do you explain how the *New York Times* and other senior national papers, and then television news, don't touch this?

VIDAL: They don't want you to know...so I would think any newspaper that wanted to feature it. What I've been chatting just now with you I was also chatting with a radio station, call-in station in Ohio, and the guy was asking me questions. He said, "All right, so where was the *New York Times*? Where's the *Washington Post*?" He said, "Very often they don't bother with us out here in the provinces, but where is the *Cleveland Plain Dealer*? Where is the *Toledo Blade*? Where are our own papers out here? They know perfectly well what's going on, much better than the *New York Times* would ever know." Silence, silence. Well, it is no secret that a very few people own most of the country, the famous one percent. Well, sometimes it's like Monopoly: They go out and buy some newspapers, they buy some TV stations, they select people to serve in Congress. Mostly their lawyers they send there, lobbyists go there. It's not meant for real people. And they've scared away most real people, who have to go through a terrible indoctrination course before they're led in to high office. They don't want bad news.

Now, I wrote the preface to Conyers's book, and the book is doing fairly well out there in blogger land, but no mention in any of the newspapers. Now, the first newspaper that runs a headline about what happened in Ohio, I think the *Nation*'s "There's Something Rotten in Ohio," they made the title of my piece. And I think the *Nation*, you know, sold three or four more copies than usual with that powerful statement on the cover. But when our media does not want to make money out of news, corruption is complete. You would think that that was something totally against nature. You don't want to sell papers; you don't want to sell washing machines or whatever you're selling on television; you don't want to sell it; you don't want to go against what the owners of the country want, and they don't want bad news of this sort, and they don't want the people really to know about these things.

JAY: And particularly don't want to take any chance of delegitimizing a sitting president. I guess they're terrified of that.

VIDAL: Well, since he wasn't legitimate to begin with, I don't see why they're disturbed about him. I mean, even he knows—you can just tell by the tricky look in his eyes—that he shouldn't be there. At least he's got this oafish manner, which has some charm to it if you like, you know, country music, and I rather do. But he doesn't have Nixon's look, which is, *Yes, I did put the poison in your well, and you just go drink it. You'll never catch my fingerprints on that—ha, ha, ha.* Well, Nixon was a real villain. I mean, he just telegraphed it. This one, it's just, "I'm wartime president, a wartime president," dancing along. I mean, there he is, you know, the wise bunny, and just kind of full of fun, whereas Kerry looked like a mortician, you know, without a corpse, but standing alone in the cemetery at the end (if I may complete this beautiful metaphor for you).

JAY: Getting back to the way big media allows the

Democrats and Republican leadership to define the barriers of debate, in the whole presidential campaign, not a word about—I love how they call what the administration did "incompetence" in relation to 9/11. At the very least one would think you would use the word "negligence," and if not "criminal negligence." Not a word about it in the entire election campaign, because when Kerry, for his own reasons, doesn't say a word, and then big media, which you would think would have been—at least alongside Iraq—the story of the election: Did you or did you not bear some responsibility for 9/11? Not a word.

VIDAL: No, because they knew they wouldn't get the word. And, the Republican managers were quite clever in demonizing Kerry. Kerry was a genuine war hero in Vietnam. So, you know, Machiavelli (if I may bring up a great Italian), Machiavelli wrote hundreds of years ago—and he's one of the best writers on politics that ever lived—he said if you want to destroy an opponent, you do it by attacking his virtues. If he's a generous man, say he's terribly mean; if he's a loving man, you say he's full of hate; if he's efficient, just say, oh, he's so sloppy. You get counter to him. Now, we have a draft dodger as president, another draft dodger as vice president. So you get a genuine war hero, and what do you say? "It's not true—we were there with him. He didn't deserve the third Purple Heart and the Bronze Star. Come on. He handed that to himself." You throw doubt on it.

Now, Kerry, instead of going to battle, just says,

"Well, I didn't see any of you people in Vietnam. Not one of you. I didn't see you, Cheney; I didn't see you, Bush; I didn't see any of you. Shall I go through the list?" And I'd go through a list of two hundred Republican politicians and let 'em squirm. You were playing it safe and letting us die for you, and you're doing it again. And now—the other subject that's not being brought up in the press, and, Lewis Lapham did in *Harper's Magazine*—the troops are deserting; they're going AWOL. We've never had this happen on such a scale. I dare not say it the last time, because the last time was with George Washington, in which every time winter came, the entire revolutionary army would go home and sit by the fire until the weather was nice. You know? And poor Washington was at his wit's end. But—except that turned out well.

But this isn't turning out well. And they can't get people to recruit. Who wants to go over there and step on land mines or be blown up by automobiles? This isn't war. This is a subject people objecting to their conquerors occupying their land and destroying their religion, their buildings, their livelihood, and stealing their oil. We, we are the bad guys there. "Oh, no! You can't say that about our brave guys and gals!" Well, we have brave guys and gals there—all the more reason to save their lives and bring them home and not leave them there to be slaughtered, which is what's happening now. These people seem to think—the Cheney-Bush gang—they seem to think they're in a bad movie. Well, admittedly, it's a lousy movie, but it's not a real movie, because these are real people being killed. They haven't grasped it. It's a game: "Boy, we got the Democrats on that one. And habeas corpus? Don't try it again. You'll stay in Guantánamo as long as we want you there, because, you see, you could be a terrorist." And they chuckle among themselves, holding innocent people. But it's—they're orgasmic with delight at how they are getting rid of the Bill of Rights and holding people who should not be held, and then blaming an innocent fool like Kerry for being a coward, when the only thing in his favor is that he was a very brave man in a war that I certainly wouldn't have volunteered to be in one of those boats.

JAY: Again, none of it was possible without television news. And more than print, because you can actually find the odd article in print.

VIDAL: In time you can find it, yes.

JAY: Yeah. But in television news, it's a wasteland, and 80 percent of people are getting their news from TV. The 1968 debate with you and Buckley—I can't imagine them, in any major news story, putting the equivalent to or the actual Gore Vidal on main network television in the midst of a major political event. It's not that television was ever wonderful, but you couldn't even imagine you or someone like you allowed that kind of platform today. So start from there.

VIDAL: Well, in 1968, when ABC decided they wanted to be number one covering the Democratic and Republican conventions, they decided to get the two

noisiest politicians, political commentators around—
Buckley and myself. And they went to the top of the
ratings. They passed—for the first time, ABC was
number one in the ratings. And Goldenson was
president then. And I remember we were in Miami
covering the Republican convention, and I'd come
down in the morning after we'd do our number at
night. And then I'd go out in the morning, and he'd be
sitting out there with all these scrolls with the numbers,
watching himself, ABC, go to number one. He said, "It's
just amazing what you boys are doing, amazing. Now
there's a falling off here at three minutes to ten. Can
you remember what you were talking about then?
Don't do it again, 'cause you dropped and CBS passed
us. But, look at this: You're back again. You must have
done something." I mean, it was that finely—they cared
about ratings; they cared about business; they cared
about their stockholders. I wouldn't say that they were
in love with truth, but at least they got two people who
they thought were telling the truth, or at least I did.
And they got big ratings.

In those days, not just 1968 for that one election, but
in those days, there were twenty talk programs, all over
the country. There was one in Philadelphia—what's his
name? I keep forgetting. There was Dick Cavett. There
was Suskind. They were on regularly, at least once a
week, twice a week, three times a week. At one point,
Suskind and I, we had the first call-in TV program. I was
the host; Suskind was the producer. And we had one
telephone. It was Dorothy Kilgallen and me, and
sometimes Suskind, and always a guest, you know,

somebody notorious. In the middle of the table was this black telephone, and the telephone would ring, and the one nearest to it, Dorothy Kilgallen, often had to—"Oh, it's for you, Gore," looking very disappointed. I'd say, "Oh, fine." I'd have to get up from my place and walk around the table to pick up the phone and talk to the caller. Well, everybody watched that thing. It was the most popular program. We did it seven nights a week, ninety minutes. And it was for the three cities, as they call it, you know, Jersey City, New York, whatever else was the third one. Well, people were fascinated not only to see the personalities up close, but to see conversation that would go off in all directions. People would reveal themselves, they'd talk about politics, and so on.

So although Buckley and I can be said to have put ABC to the number one slot during the two conventions, there was already a tradition of free speech, very free speech. And there were people— even in those days Mike Wallace was interesting with his *Nightline*, which he would—"Are you really a pedophile, sir? Everyone knows. You might just as well admit it here." Puffing smoke in your face, you know. But it was a different world.

JAY: But if you'd been on, the night of the elections, say, as one of the pundits, any network that had you on and debating an equivalent of a Buckley, it would have been exploded. They would have cleaned up. At least half the country that voted for the Democrats would have watched that channel and not the others. And they didn't ask you, or an equivalent of you—if there is one, I'm not sure—but they didn't go, as you're saying, for what would have been a good, clear business decision, for their own political reasons.

VIDAL: No, their own political reasons are all-important, and they don't care about the shareholders, they don't care about making money. They want propaganda, they want big money, and big money is having the Pentagon in your pocket and being able to sell them weapons. General Electric makes nuclear weapons; it owns NBC. Is NBC going to talk about an overrun at General Electric? No, they're not going to talk about it. But I might if they got me on, so just keep him off.

At ABC, Peter Jennings, a very young kid just in from Canada, was my gopher for the sixty-eight debates. And we became friends. I've seen him up until this recent illness. Every four years since 1968, or since he came to power, he would go to the head of programming and say, "Let's get Gore on for the elections." "No way." And he even appealed to them, "After all, that's how you got to be number one, which you'd never been before in anything, for those debates." "No." And he would say, "Well, why not?" 'Cause I was still going on television. I was quite visible around the world, certainly around the country. They said, "He'll just be outrageous." "Well, having been on four or five shows, you know, the previous week, well, outrageous in what sense? Was he outrageous on Suskind? Was he outrageous on Cavett?" "Well, that's not the point." You see, he never got a straight answer, because they couldn't give one.

Our owners are after big military contracts; they're after rehabilitation in Iraq or Vietnam or wherever we happen to be waging a war. "This guy doesn't seem to like our wars; he doesn't appreciate what we're doing for freedom and democracy for people everywhere in the world. This guy's got no heart. Vidal has no heart. He doesn't weep when he thinks of all the wickedness that Saddam Hussein has inflicted on his own people." This comes out now in just one sentence, and very fast, to which the answer is, well, isn't that his people's business and his business and not your business? The United States was not appointed guardian of the Iraqi people. But there we are, and they really love it too, don't they?

JAY: They've been able to close down the whole discussion and analysis and look at 9/11.

VIDAL: Well, there is so much—there are so many questions that they refuse to answer. There are so many questions that television refuses to take up, much less answer. There are things they don't want to talk about. Nine/eleven is filled with questions. Why, for instance—it is the law of the land, if a plane is hijacked, fighter planes are scrambled, I think it's within two and a half minutes from the nearest airbase, and there—all air bases in the U.S., they're pretty close to wherever a domestic airliner might be hijacked. They were not scrambled, as they call it, they were not put up in the air. Why not? Well, you can't blame people for saying they must have been ordered to stand down, not to go up and stop the hijackers from hitting the Pentagon. This is the center of the Empire; this is the muscle of the American Empire. They'd rather sacrifice that and continue playing whatever game it was they were playing, which meant they didn't want to do anything about the hijackers at that point. Then they declare war on terrorism, which is an abstract noun. That's not much help.

JAY: At the very least, it's not even debatable that George Bush was told by George Tenet seven months before 9/11 that the number one security threat to the United States was al-Qaeda and Osama bin Laden; it's not debatable that Condoleezza Rice got a memo saying, Osama bin Laden plans to attack the United States; and in both cases, as far as we know, did nothing after both of these alerts. That's not even a matter of factual controversy. Yet that's not a story. It's just dropped.

VIDAL: Well, that gives rise to conspiracy theories. Now, like everyone else, I get pretty bored by some of the fantastic conspiracy theories that are inflicted upon us, sometimes I think deliberately. By and large I think one thing most people sense that they've been shamed into not admitting they sense it: Everything in the United States is a conspiracy. What is a political party but a conspiracy to raise an awful lot of money and steal an election or win it honestly or just buy it outright? That's a conspiracy. Democrats conspire.

Republicans conspire. General Motors conspires to send out these trucks that seem to explode or whatever it is they're doing now. Everybody is conspiring.

How did we get like this? We got like this because the only art form that we ever created and perfected was the television commercial. We have nothing else to our credit as a civilization. To try and persuade people to buy things that they don't need that are probably bad for them and may blow up in their face, and to cover up everything that's wrong with what you're obliging people to buy. Well, once they found out how easy it was to sell a detergent which costs about half a penny to make a box of, why not sell the next president in the same way and make him just as phony as the detergent? So everybody's brought up with TV advertising from childhood, and the first thing a baby is told: "Well, I want to send away for the magic ring that will make me invisible"—"Oh, that's just advertising." Well, every child learns that one—it's just advertising. Then they see a presidential candidate. Well, of course, that's just talk. So everybody's wise to the conspiracies, but they don't think of them as sinister; they think of them just—it's just, you know, a lot of bull. Well, it's more than that. It cost us two elections, presidential elections. We may not have that many more in which to express our will. It has got the Congress in the hands of the most extraordinary people I've ever seen there, and I was brought up in Washington in the center of that world. There's never been anything quite as crazy as that meeting of the judiciary committee when the

Republicans drove the Democrats out of the chamber and began giggling and winking, and showing off into the cameras, and then switching the audio off so that they couldn't be heard after the Republicans sneaked out of the meeting. Nothing like that could have happened when we were a real country, but we're not. We're owned by a small group of corporate Americans. They know what they want, they're getting what they want, and they've got their eye now on the last gold rush of them all: Social Security. To grab that money will be the triumph of this gang. And they'll probably all go and live in Samoa.

JAY: Talk about the psychology of the American people who suffer, most of them. Many are poor. Many live with economic insecurity. And not all are Buffalo. Most of the big cities voted against Bush. But just give us a bit of the landscape of and what you think—how can this, will this sort of hold the mythology has on people's minds?

VIDAL: Well, in the long run, it's the control over a country by a ruling class, elite, whatever word you want to use. It's done through manipulation of, essentially, information, or what appears to be information. If you control the media, then you've pretty much got it. We were such a big country; there was so much media; there was such a long distance between the *LA Times*, the *New York Times*; there was three thousand miles and different mentalities in both places. Now it's more homogenized between cable and network. Place gets smaller and smaller.

Traditionally, the American people have been antiwar and anti-imperial. We were pro-expansion when it was just North America. We wanted all of it, or at least all the central part, and we locked up what we call the Indians on reservations. And then my grandfather came along and invented something called Oklahoma, which put the Indians back, once again, at poverty level. So we kept taking away the lands that we'd given them. But essentially when it came to foreign wars, we were not eager to go. World War I, Woodrow Wilson found ways of jazzing it up so that—horror stories, mostly in the press, mostly about what the Kaiser was doing: They were raping nuns in Belgium; they were skewering babies on bayonets. I mean, it was ferocious propaganda. And interesting that it worked, because the largest single white minority in the United States is German—and they were very patriotic, a lot of them, I mean for the old country. But they turned them around, and we went into World War I.

World War II, I was an isolationist then, as was Senator Gore, my grandfather. Eighty percent of the country did not want to go and fight in Europe, no matter how bad Hitler was. And contrary to what we hear, we knew nothing about what he was doing to the Jews in 1940, which was the crucial year of decision. Then Japanese are maneuvered into attacking us, and we're at war again. I spent three years in the Pacific, and you know, I never heard one patriotic word from any soldier, American soldier. It was none of this, "Oh, gee. I just love Old Glory. Every time I see it go by," that movie stuff. It was just, you know, "This is—isn't this the most awful damned thing?" And, you know, "Joe got killed, and so-and-so has lost a leg." And it was a bloodbath, particularly for the marines. I was not in the marines, thank God, but they took terrible casualties because they had the world's worst officers, who believed in just throwing them into battle, throwing them into battle, throwing them into battle. We were going to suffocate the Japanese with our dead bodies.

So you have a people that basically wants to mind its own business. It's a people easily manipulated by public opinion. We're terrified of public opinion from the moment we're born, partly due to religious training, partly due to an educational system that is not very interested in educating us. What, really, the rulers want are docile workers, who refuse to have anything to do with minimum wage or labor unions, and passionate consumers—they got to buy all that junk that they're advertising, and they do. So in general that—or, I'd say the average American is a very peaceful sort of person, rather very shrewd about his own interests, which is why it takes advertising genius, which we have (we invented advertising genius) to get him to vote against his own interest time after time again. You see them, those people, coming out to vote for Bush a second time. All of his crimes—by then, most of them were known: his incompetence, if you want to be polite about it, at the time of 9/11; his running away from responsibility; his throwing us into a war that's unconstitutional without a declaration by Congress. I mean, the whole thing was enough to turn—but people just sort of forgave him: "Well, he's the president." And he was so happy, going around, "I'm wartime president, I'm wartime president." And he just—you know, he seemed just cute as a bug's ear. Well, then we got the rest of the bug, and that's not a good bug.

JAY: And people are scared.

VIDAL: They were scared by 9/11. And then you see they got to work with the big lie that Saddam Hussein was working with al-Qaeda and Osama bin Laden. Everybody knows who knows anything about it. I mean just anybody who reads the European press knows that the two men hated each other and had nothing to do with each other. But if you're president and vice president, one on Monday will say that they worked together for 9/11, on Tuesday the other one will say it. They just go back and forth. Repetition, repetition, repetition. What's that? The secret of advertising: Rinso White, Rinso White, Rinso White. That's how it's done. And we were Rinso-wedded into the wars. And nobody went willingly, I can tell you that. I mean, there are people who certainly got jazzed up by it all, and there are people who certainly were upset, as well they should be, by what was done at 9/11 to us.

JAY: But there is also, is there not, a religion of Americanism that people do believe in? And also an extension of some of the forms of Christian belief, where Americanism is almost inseparable from the

Christianity of it or the other parts of the religious belief?

VIDAL: I don't think there are many true believers in Americanism. I belong to what is now being called the "greatest generation." I can tell you that I, as I said—I was in the army three years, mostly in the Pacific, and I never heard a patriotic word from any fellow soldiers. They just hated the war and they didn't want to be there. They also knew that they're being thrown away, particularly the marines, these god-awful officers were throwing them just wave after wave after wave onto entrenched Japanese, and they were being slaughtered. And they all knew that back home a lot of people were making a lot of money, not to mention getting off with their girlfriends. And there was a lot of violent feeling against our rulers among the soldiers in that war. And so it went.

Roosevelt knew pretty much what he was doing, and he realized that he wanted peace. He made an accommodation at Yalta with Stalin, which Truman proceeded to break every arrangement that Roosevelt had set up for a peaceful coexistence with Stalin. And Truman thought that it would be a good idea, and he was advised on this by Charles E. Wilson. But why—after these wars come—why not just stay armed all the time, thinking about all the money that would be for the military budget each year, and how good that would be for General Electric, for General Motors, and General MacArthur? So the generals were heard from—the industrial generals—and we have remained armed ever since.

Well, you can't justify all this money being thrown away. Well, nothing is going to education, nothing to health care. You can't justify it unless you find an enemy. Well, there are plenty of enemies if you look around for them, and we found them. Imagine invading Panama. Somebody explained at the time—that was Bush Sr.—"That was to get Noriega, because he was in charge of all the drugs in the world. Oh my God—we've got to stop him. He's a man of such evil, such evil." So the big propaganda machine begins. Well, he was not in charge of much of anything. And we went in and we knocked down—we killed quite a few Panamanians. And an old Washington hand heard directly from somebody in Bush's administration, "Why on earth did you go out to Panama? That looked very bad in the eyes of the world." "Well, we did it because we could." That's their attitude.

JAY: In your memoirs, you talk about how, early on, you amongst others believed in the myths of the Cold War, and then you started to see through how much of that was mythology. Can you talk about that?

VIDAL: Well, I think I saw through the myths of the Cold War almost from the beginning. I was a Washington political kid from a political family. My grandfather did not like Roosevelt, whom I quite admired. I mean, I was a born New Dealer and he was a right-wing Democrat. But he knew quite a lot about what was going on, and he knew perfectly well that

Roosevelt had set us up for Pearl Harbor. He forced the Japanese with an ultimatum. Nineteen forty-one, I think it was in November, he sent them an ultimatum: "Get out of China." They'd been trying to conquer China for eight years. They got as far as Manchuria. "If you don't, we will turn off your oil supply." They were getting all their oil for their airplanes and so on from us, and scrap metal, which they were getting from us. They had no natural resources of that kind. He just backed them up. Why did he do it? Well, he couldn't get—he wanted us to go to war to save England and France. France had fallen to the Nazis. England was being battered to pieces by the German aircraft. American people would not go to war. He wanted a replay of 1917: Germans sank some of our ships; therefore he had an occasion— Woodrow Wilson had an occasion to go to war. They did the same thing again: The Germans sank several of our ships. Roosevelt sat back and, "Well, that'll do it. Public opinion. They'll want war." Americans said, "We don't want it. We got burnt in 1917. We're not going back. We're not going over, over there." What to do?

Well, we were already struggling with Japan in the Pacific, who was to be the master of the Pacific. My father, the director of air commerce, was already starting to build bases on places like Howland Island, the so-called Guana Islands, which we seized from the British. My father was very funny in the newsreels about that. My father said, "You know, I looked at the map before we took those islands to put in landing strips"— this was to get ready for the Pacific war with Japan— "and, you know, the British Empire's all pink. Well, you know, this part wasn't pink," said my father, talking to *The March of Time*, "so I thought it was an empty Guano Island." My father had a great sense of humor, and he knew it was a great comedy number that he was doing for the president. We were getting ready for that war. And by switching off everything, that's an ultimatum. The Japanese had nothing left but to hit us, which they did at Pearl Harbor. Roosevelt had sort of thought they'd hit Manila, which was much closer to them, less damaging to us. So he was stunned by how enormous it was and was afraid that he'd be impeached.

Now, you had a senator for a grandfather, you know exactly what's going on in the cloakroom and how they were talking impeachment. And Roosevelt was just maneuvering as quickly as possible to say, you know, "Japanese are coming, Japanese are coming. Subhuman people. Lock 'em up."

JAY: Roosevelt was afraid of a victorious German-Japanese empire encircling the United States, and then being the empire of the second half of the century.

VIDAL: Well, I think that being the empire was on his mind for the United States. See, we had picked the war with Spain, from which we grabbed the Philippines, which was their territory, their colony. So we were already a Pacific power. And we were sitting on the edge of China. China was breaking up. Japan was suddenly becoming militaristic, trying to take over China. Germany was making awful noises too that they wouldn't mind a piece of China. So Roosevelt—

Roosevelt also, to his credit, realized that Hitler was something new. This wasn't the Kaiser; this was a new element that really should be stopped. How do you explain that to the people who haven't been told anything about him other than they've got this funny little guy, looks like Charlie Chaplin? So there was no way—it was too late to educate by then. But you could maneuver the Japanese into hitting you. Then you have to make reprisal. And many people think that has been a pattern with us ever since, to get people to strike at us first.

JAY: So the war ends. America is on the verge of being the empire. And the Cold War. Talk about the national security state and what follows. And also, even just from your own understanding of it, how it unfolded.

VIDAL: Well, it unfolded rapidly. The joker in the deck was Roosevelt's death. Everyone who knew him, including my father, knew he was dying and that his last—he was elected president, what, four times? And the last race, it was clear that he was a dying man. But he had all his marbles, and he had them, all of his marbles, at Yalta. He got more out of Stalin than Stalin got out of him. It's only a right-wing Republican who'll say, "Oh, Roosevelt was really a communist, you know." Well, it's because he came from a much higher class than these Republicans do. They hadn't seen an American aristocrat, nor did they know how tough they are, and Roosevelt was a tough one, and he was imperial-minded.

He had been brought up with the dominance of the British Empire. He hated the British Empire. He had a scene with Churchill right after Yalta—I guess at the time of Yalta—when he said, "You know, when this thing is over"—and it was pretty clear that Germany was about to fold—he said, "When this is over, you've got to let India go." And Churchill said, "As we've always known, one day," and so on. And Roosevelt said, "Not one day—you're letting them go right away, and the French are going to get out of Indochina, the Dutch are going to get out of Java, and we're getting rid of all the colonial empires. And Roosevelt knew in the back of his mind who will inherit them—we will. And Churchill was—thought that this guy was his friend. Emperor have no friends. And finally Churchill said—it was at a dinner party, a lot of people witnessed this scene—he said, "Well, do you want me to get up on my hind legs like your little dog Fala and beg?" And the emperor said, "Yes." And that's when Churchill knew what he was up against: A new Emperor Augustus was on the scene, and he was an American.

Then he drops dead, and the most incompetent little man you could dream of succeeds him. Well, behind him was a very brilliant man called Dean Acheson, who was the secretary of state, who did know about the empire and did understand how the world worked. So Acheson—he could play Truman like a harmonica, and he got Truman overexcited by Stalin and communism and how evil it was. Truman fell for all of it, or he pretended to. So they said, "Well, Russia's on the march." They'd lost twenty million people; where are they going to march to? They could barely get out of Middle Europa. They didn't have enough gas or enough tanks to take their canons, their artillery back to Russia; they had to have horses drag them back. I mean, they were just about finished. And yet we start this thing, the Russians are coming. So we divide Germany, and then we say the Russians did it. We did the division. We gave them the worst part, the east, the old Prussian part; we took the west and the Ruhr and all the rich part of Germany. We turn them into our ally. We started to rearm them. I mean, that just drove many people crazy: "After Hitler, you're going to rearm the Germans?" And yeah. Well, Truman thought it was a good idea. And then he devised the national security state.

Now, the national security state had about seven points to it. One was never negotiate honestly with Russians. Two was total rearmament and constant rearmament and develop the hydrogen bomb because they were going to get the atomic bomb one day. In other words, you created a totally militarized economy, which we are to this day. That was the—that's the end result. Then, along the way, Potsdam, where Truman went trying to con Stalin into helping us defeat Japan, which was not yet finished. As soon as he gets there, he gets a telegram: The atom bomb works. Now, Harry Truman hadn't been told about it; he just learned about it. It works. What should we do? All of his commanders, from Eisenhower to Admiral Nimitz in the Pacific, said under no circumstances drop this bomb on the Japanese. They are begging for peace. There's not a building standing in Tokyo; it's all paper cities, all burned up. You will be hated by all the world. And it was Eisenhower who was the most furious about this. That's one of the reasons he hated Truman to the end of his days. Truman just wanted to look like Little Napoleon, and he said—he dropped it twice. Thus we earn the hatred of much of the world, because at least Asia knew that the Japanese had been defeated by us. Totally defeated. We were spreading the word that it would cost one million American lives to invade Japan. Well, it would if there'd been a Japanese army there, but what was left of it was in China, and they didn't have any boats to get across the water from mainland Asia back to their island. Everything was phony. And that is how we got started on our imperial militaristic course was under Truman. And, naturally, they write books about this folksy nice little guy who just loved his daughter and got upset when she got bad reviews for her singing.

JAY: So the development of the national security state, the increased militarization of the economy, and then you have this sort of political, ideological charge, I guess to some extent led by the revered Senator McCarthy. Talk a bit about the political, ideological, commercial-advertising-type of transformation that accompanied these developments.

VIDAL: Well, to militarize the United States totally in every sense was a great challenge for our advertisers. And Senator Vandenberg—kind of a goose in the Senate, but a canny Republican, so Harry Truman needed him. When Truman announced the national security state and this huge military buildup in peacetime, we were on top of the world: Japan was finished and nuclearized; Germany was occupied, divided in half. So Vandenberg said, "Well, I agree with you about the menace of communism. But if you're going to get, after this long and expensive war, the money you want for a buildup, you're going to have to scare the hell out of the American people." And Truman took on the job, and he did. And the only person to stand up against him was the true heir of Franklin Roosevelt, and that was former Vice President Wallace.

The tragedy was of course the succession to Roosevelt. His personal choice, and that of the New Dealers, which was the heart and soul of the Democratic Party, was Henry Wallace. But he got smeared by the media, who had other plans, and they wanted a little conservative fellow from the Midwest— Harry Truman—and they just thought life would be safer with him. Wallace they thought was a wild-eyed reformer. He was a reformer, but he was not wild-eyed. Anyway, he was replaced by Harry Truman. Roosevelt, it was his last term, and he was not paying much attention by then.

So now this totally unprepared little guy is now emperor of the world. The global empire is in place. Luckily for him, so he didn't make too many mistakes, he had Dean Acheson, who was a super-diplomat, very smooth figure, and knew his history. So they begin. Wallace knows what's happening. Truman uses the threat of the Soviet Union allegedly against Yugoslavia, which is part of the Communist Bloc, and Turkey, not, and began to make threatening noises to Stalin and the Russians—"Don't you dare"—and Greece. "Don't you dare. Greece is our part of the world," and so forth and so on. Stalin said, "We're—we have no interest in Greece." You know. Tito in Yugoslavia was inclining toward us, anyway.

However, it looked like we might be ready for war, so, therefore, all the money was appropriated by Senator Vandenberg for a new building, which they'd just finished (I think then), that was called the Pentagon. And what had been the old War Department ever since George Washington, all through my period in the army, was now the Department of Defense, which is wildly funny, because it's been nothing but offense ever since. Then the CIA was invented out of the remains of the old OSS, which was the information-collecting aspect of the War Department. We were setting up a military empire all around the world. We had bases everywhere.

Jim Forrestal, who was secretary of the navy and then became secretary of defense, and then went mad and jumped out a window at Walter Reed Hospital, having just read *Ajax* by a Greek—a Greek tragedian. It was a very spooky time. He said, "Wherever—" He said, "Well, how many more bases do you want?" This is when he was still secretary of the navy. "Wherever there's water," he said, "there'll be an American ship." Then the air force suddenly said, "You know, the British

Isles are at great risk when the Russians start marching across Europe, as they will do." Nobody had any evidence they were going to do it. "So just to be safe, we're going to send some B-29 bombers with atomic warheads so the British Isles will be safe from the Russians." And that was the first time that England has ever been occupied since the Norman invasion. And those planes are still there. I don't think they have atomic warheads anymore, but B-29s just stayed and stayed and stayed. And the word around the War Department, Pentagon, was, "Well, they've got to get used to our presence everywhere." So now the Empire is in full flow.

Then out of it came—Truman, in his un-wisdom, decided to straighten things. There were critics at home, some of them very brilliant. He had to shut them up. So Truman insisted on loyalty oaths from everybody in government, from the janitor to the secretary of state. They must swear that they were not communists, they would never collaborate with communism, no matter where, what, so forth. Nothing like that had ever been done to American citizens. Wallace went on the attack and said, "Now, Mr. Truman has declared war on the rest of the world, and we are to protect any regime, no matter how terrible, if it says it's anti-communist. We're ringing the world with bases to no end, to no practical end, but great expense. And he's creating fear wherever he goes." The entire media went to work: "Henry A. Wallace is a communist." He then, in 1948, ran as an independent for president, would have done terribly well, all of the brighter people in the country voted for him, but he was so smeared as a communist, and they had so many wild stories about him, and that he went to a swami for instruction in Indian lore, I mean, this was the nonsense that went on.

So now there is no voice to speak against Harry Truman and Dean Acheson, who spoke well enough for both of them. So now we are at the gate, we have crossed the Rubicon, we have got through the Great Wall of China. The American Empire is in business, and let anybody try and upset it. The Koreans did. Korea decided—they misunderstood something Acheson said. Acheson had seemed to say in a speech—because he was telling the world—everything belonged to us. He left out North Korea. South Korea said, "See? They have everything else. They have South Korea, but they don't have North Korea. So let's unite with them again, since we were one country to begin with." So we had nothing but green troops up there, kids that had just been drafted, and they handed us our head. Now, Harry Truman didn't dare go to Congress and ask for a declaration of war, because he probably wouldn't have got it so soon after World War II. So he goes to the United Nations (irony, irony) and asks for a police action for the Americans to take against Korea, against the North Koreans, who are now being backed up by Mao Tse-tung, by the Chinese. Now, here we are at a big—potentially a lethal—large Asian war for the sake of the empire. We had no national interest at all. If the two Koreas had come together, what—no one, no one cared, really, but it was all showing off, showing off. Me, macho; you, sissy. And it was that game.

So we—we lost that one. We pretended we won it, and MacArthur at the Inchon landing did a great piece of military maneuvering, which is the last that he ever did. He came back to speak to Congress, 'cause it was a great move to—people thought—to running for president, 'cause Truman by then had just dropped to nothing. He was blamed for the Korean War, for our failure for this or that. And my father was a friend of MacArthur—my father was an instructor at West Point when he was superintendent. So my father, you know, welcomed him home, and MacArthur made a great speech to Congress, and expected immediately to be hailed as the next president. Nothing happened. So my father called him up a couple of days later and had lunch with MacArthur, and then he said, "Well, that was a great speech. Are you going to run for president?" He said, "Well, I was willing to, but nobody came even to thank me for the speech [*laughs*]. So I guess I have to go home." So that's how we lost President MacArthur.

Meanwhile, the empire is chugging along, Harry Truman eventually goes away, and we get Dwight Eisenhower, who said quite—did a number of good things, a number of bad things, but he did say he saw that the military were getting away with everything, and he said, "Thank God we have a president (me) who understands the military, and they'll steal everything in sight, and these civilians don't know anything about it, and everything they ask for they're getting, and we'll be bankrupt by the time they finish." So Eisenhower at least held back the Pentagon.

JAY: Tell us that famous Eisenhower statement about the military–industrial complex. What's the story behind it?

VIDAL: In the interest of British oil, which Mosaddeq in Iran was putting a tax on—they never paid a penny to the Iranian government; Mosaddeq felt they should at least pay their way—there was an alarm call from the British government: We must do something about it. So Theodore Roosevelt's son was put in charge of the overthrow of Prime Minister Mosaddeq, which we did, ridding them of a very good government, and their hatred for us began with that interference in their affairs. And we could have lived happily with Mosaddeq. He also, 1953, he also did the same thing in Guatemala to the democratically elected government of Árbenz. Two bad things that he did.

The good thing was, upon—he kept back military spending. And then, when he left office, he made this great speech, and he explained why it was necessary to have such a huge military. Might have been better if he'd said we don't need this much military for our task in the world to preserve freedom for ourselves. But he said no matter how necessary, and we think it is, that we have this great military–industrial complex, it is a dangerous thing because of the vast amounts of federal money that are going to private corporations for our defense—and he was trying have it both ways—which is necessary, which is necessary. And he said this is going to change everything in the way our country's governed: It's going to change us politically; it'll change us spiritually. And then part of the speech which I've always loved, nobody ever quotes it. After all, he'd been president of Columbia University. He said the effect of all this money coming to our universities, even though it's for the physics department, the nuclear departments, is going to affect all education. And if the universities are not the home of free investigation, suddenly our knowledge of the world is curtailed by this huge amount of money, which will control the responses of everybody, including the history department. He didn't say that, but that was his meaning.

So that's how that started. Did anybody pay attention? No, they didn't. He went off and played golf. Kennedy kept on with the imperial, you know, on the march, "bear any burden," so forth, and so on. And then he had his unfortunate—unfortunate death, and we got Lyndon Johnson.

Hollywood and Washington

JAY: The political importance of Hollywood as a vehicle of political public opinion seemed to have been important, but partly, I guess, because of how strong progressive Hollywood was during the war, and then so targeted by McCarthy. Can you just talk a bit about that, and then take us a bit forward in history in terms of Hollywood in politics?

VIDAL: Well, Hollywood in Washington had always seemed to me (since I spent a good deal of time in both, and both politics and movies), it was a symbiotic relationship: They both—they both deal with illusions, and reality doesn't often play much of a part in fictional narratives, which is, after all, what we do in a movie on the screen and what we do with a candidate in politics. And they belong together.

The first person to realize that was Woodrow Wilson. Odd, because he was a rather highbrow professor of English, history, but literary minded. And when he was trying to get us into World War I, well, you had to get Hollywood aboard, to get them to make movies demonizing the Germans. Press was doing a good job, and again, those raped nuns and babies spitted on bayonets and so forth, it was a great deal of anti-German propaganda coming out.

He was a great admirer, by the way, of *Birth of a Nation*; he was also a tremendous anti-black racist. This didn't come out until much later in his regime. But he always—he had a feeling—he loved *Birth of a Nation* because it proved every racist theory he had, so D. W. Griffith he'd studied. Now, he's trying to get America into a warlike mood to go to Europe to fight the Kaiser in order to help England and help us too in the wrong—in some ways. But he had to get Hollywood going. But he'd seen the effect—he was so affected by *Birth of a Nation*, he got a guy called George Creel, who was a big PR man long before PR had been invented.

This guy was superb. He was magazine writer, I think he ran a magazine, and he was a great propagandist. He hired George Creel to go to Hollywood and be the president's ambassador. Creel went out there, met the movie makers, persuaded them to make movies about the Hun, the savage Hun, the crimes of the Hun, and a whole series of movies were made demonizing the Germans. There are at least two pictures that I know of in which Woodrow Wilson, the sitting president of the United States, appears, and somebody will say, "Oh, by the way, here comes President Wilson." "Good evening, ladies and gentlemen. I am President Wilson." And he'd shake a hand. And he ended the plot: "And I want to commend you for bravery as a nun against the Huns," and he'd pin a medal on. It's gorgeous, dumb stuff. And that was the beginning. And Hollywood never looked back. Or forward. And every president since has known that the movies, if you could harness them, was the way to get your program across, particularly if you wanted to go to war.

That was the way to get people excited. Roosevelt

first had radio because he had this great speaking voice, and everyone liked to hear the president. "Tonight..." I'll never forget this one on radio. You'll never hear this again from a president. But Singapore had just fallen to the Japanese. "Tonight, the news is all bad." Well, at that moment the entire country will help you, Mr. President. You know. "We want the news to be good for America again." Oh, God, how he played the people, and he's superb.

Then newsreels came along. He proved to be just as good at newsreels as he was as a voice, and he used to call them his garbos. And you'll see him sitting at his desk: "Well, my dog little Fala has joined me here. You can see him sitting at the corner. He'll join us in a minute." And he played—he had the little dog, he had his grandchildren, he had Eleanor. I mean, it was just glorious stuff. And H. L. Mencken was very funny on the subject.

Mencken was a great skeptic about Roosevelt, found him entirely phony, but he was entirely beguiling and charming, and he got the New Deal through, and he got the Japanese into the war, built up the fleet and the air force that defeated the Germans and the Japanese. He's our first emperor. And he, through—he did it through radio and he did it through newsreels in those days, which would be like television now. He would have been just as good on TV, except they wouldn't let him on, because he said substantive things. "We're sorry, Mr. President, but this is not the message that Westinghouse wants to put out, so just don't say we have nothing to fear but fear itself, because fear is what we peddle." And that is what they do peddle now.

The difference between Roosevelt and Truman, his successor, is enormous. Roosevelt's—in his first inauguration says, "We have nothing to fear but fear itself." Then comes Harry Truman: "There's a power, a monolithic power, in the world today. That power is communism, forever on the march." And he's frightening us about this terrible enemy called Russia and communism. Just—so the difference is night and day, night and day. Roosevelt had the affirmative side and swept a nation. Truman got us deeper and deeper into great trouble and stirred the pot, and out of the pot comes McCarthy, out of it comes the House Un-American Activities Committee, out of it comes, "You're not a good American. You were seen reading a book without moving your lips. That is a sure sign of a communist. And I speak as a U.S. senator." That was the game.

A number of things happened right after our victory, VE Day we called it, Victory in Europe Day, 1945, followed a few months later by VJ Day, Victory over Japan. Of the many things that happened after victory was declared over Japan, victory in Europe over the Nazis, the world looked in order, Roosevelt, the master politician, had made an alliance with Stalin.

Stalin, contrary to the propaganda, which was necessary later for reasons I shall get to, wanted to be a normal country with other normal countries. And he knew perfectly well that his system might work for an earlier generation of Russians, but it was not going to work for modern Russians. And he was a bad man. You know, the world is filled with bad men, but he was a superlative leader, Czar of all the Russians. And he got on with Roosevelt. He understood Roosevelt. Roosevelt understood him. They were both emperors, and they were both continental powers. Now, that's a great difference from an island power like England. If you live on an island, you think one way. And if you have a whole continent as we had (North America), I mean, he had an even bigger continent. He had all of central Asia, Siberia. The two emperors from the continents had more in common than they had with the island people or the people in the little countries like little Germany and little France. So they had hit it off, and they had a number of agreements which would have made Russia much more civilized, modern, less tyrannous place. And Roosevelt dies. And, suddenly Harry Truman, who understands nothing about international politics, he was the last-minute choice for vice president by Roosevelt, who was trying to sooth the right wing of the Democratic Party, particularly the south, which was racist and Democratic, as it is now racist and Republican. Roosevelt felt he had to hold on to that to hold on to Congress, so he said, "I'll get rid of Henry Wallace"—Henry Wallace had been his liberal vice president, an intelligent and worldly man—and replaced him with Harry Truman, who had many virtues and many demerits, one being he just didn't know what he was doing in the big league. And he's backed by a clever international lawyer called Dean Acheson, who was very empire-minded. So everything starts to go wrong with Roosevelt's death, and it was just fast like that. And there were no preparations.

Truman and his group were afraid that we would fall back into the Depression, which had started up again in 1939, and by 1940 was really very bad; more unemployment, practically, than there'd been in 1933. So Truman and his counselors decided that we must remain militarized, forever at war. So expensive in 1940, militarizing the country, to have to do it a second time in case something went wrong. So the decision was made to permanently militarize the United States for all time or for any foreseeable future. So a lot of people were relieved: "Well, at least we'll have full employment, as we had during the war years."

JAY: Just for kids that don't know, what had happened after World War I in terms of militarization, mobilization, and the fact there was a demobilization?

VIDAL: Well, after World War I, we were not as militarized as we were after World War II. World War II was the greatest military buildup the world had ever seen, and we did it practically overnight—something of a miracle. After World War I, we were militarized, but it wasn't that much, it wasn't that much of a war, and we were only in it briefly, 1917 in and out, though we took a lot of losses (the American people did not enjoy that). And we got nothing out of it (and the American people didn't enjoy that either). However, there was unemployment, and people didn't know what to do with the unemployed. That's where we hear about the hobos. Well, the hobos were the guys who rode the rails of the railroads across the country just looking for work. And then of course came the Depression. And I can remember veterans selling apples in the street. And then I remember when the bonus army—they wanted a bonus for having been in the war. Congress wouldn't give it to them, so they marched on Washington. And I remember, "The boners are coming, the boners are coming." I thought they were, you know, it was Halloween; I thought they were skeletons that we were going to have an army of skeletons marching up Pennsylvania Avenue. Everybody's scared. They marched on the Capitol. I drove down to the Senate with my grandfather, and somebody recognized him, they knew he was against giving them a bonus, and they heaved a rock through his car. And I saw, well, well, well, you know, we could have a revolution here— this is as close as we'd come. So the bonus army marching on to Washington with the veterans out of work, with no Roosevelt to think up jobs, to think up something for people to do.

JAY: The main point was that after World War I there was a demobilization in a different way than after World War II.

VIDAL: After World War I, they were just let go. Everybody went home. No preparations had been made. Nobody knew what, really, to do. All they knew was that the Depression had not ended three years earlier. It only ended in 1940 when Roosevelt put eight billion dollars—.

JAY: Back up to after World War I, 1917.

VIDAL: At the end of World War I, 1917, we were still in a sort of depression. We had not been in great economic health. But there was a big boost in spending, hence the so-called Roaring Twenties. A lot of people making a lot of money, and a lot of people weren't making anything. There was nothing much for people to do. So there was real terror what to do with the soldiers that had been let go. They were very angry. They wanted a bonus for having fought overseas. Congress wouldn't give it to them. They marched on Washington. General MacArthur, who was commanding general of our army, came out and confronted them with guns. People were injured. They had occupied the Anacostia Flats, which is in the far end of the District of Columbia, which had been pretty much an African American enclave. Suddenly it was filled up with veterans from all over the United States. And there is General MacArthur and his aide, Dwight D. Eisenhower, Major Eisenhower from West Point, and they are under orders from President Hoover to send these guys back home. So the government was frightened.

Then comes the boom, the 1920s, the Roaring Twenties. Then comes 1929, the bust, the thirty-two Depression, the thirty-three Roosevelt's "We have nothing to fear but fear itself"—he's now president. At first he created jobs, so it looked like everything was going to be all right, and then suddenly the Depression came back. Thirty-nine was worse than ever. Nineteen forty—and this was the fatal move, but it was the necessary move—Roosevelt put eight billion dollars—such a tiny amount to today's world—eight billion dollars into rearming, because he was suspicious.

Eight billion. He put eight billion dollars into rearming, and really arming, because we had—we didn't have an air fleet. Thanks to Lindberg—he sent Lindberg—everybody thinks Lindberg was a traitor who liked Hitler. Well, he was neither a traitor, nor did he like Hitler. Roosevelt had sent him to take a look at the Luftwaffe as an expert and just say how strong are the Germans and what about their fighter planes and their bombers. Could they attack us? Lindberg came back terrified. He said, "Look, the Germans are so far ahead of anything we've got, they're ahead of France and Britain combined." So it was Lindberg who persuaded Roosevelt to build the B-17, the Flying Fortress. He said, "This is one thing, if we start building it right now, we can have air supremacy; and if we don't have that, we can't win a war in the event there would be a war." He was an isolationist. So with that piece of fortune and good luck and prescience, thanks to Lindberg, thanks to Roosevelt, the Depression was gone, we were rearmed, and in due course were hit by Japan.

There was a world war. People have quite forgotten the Germans declared war on us; we did not declare war on them. They had an arrangement with Japan, but it was only defensive: that if either Japan or Germany was attacked by the United States or Britain or France, the Axis powers, which meant Japan, Italy, and Germany, would come to each other's aid. Hitler in a moment of perfect madness used Pearl Harbor as an excuse to declare war on the United States. . . . He cut his throat. And at the Nuremberg Trial, there was a wonderful exchange between Ribbentrop, who had been his foreign minister and Justice Jackson, who was one of the inquisitors for the American side. They had all the Nazi leaders in the dock. Jackson asks, "Why did you declare war on the United States?" He said, "Well, we had the Tripartite Treaty with Germany and Japan and Italy." And Jackson said, "I understand that, but that was defensive; this is offensive. So why did you declare war?" And Ribbentrop said, "Well, after all, a treaty is sacred." And Jackson just—"Yes, I know that, but since you broke every other treaty you ever made with anyone on earth, why did you observe the one treaty which would destroy you?" No answer to that one. Ribbentrop was not the brightest light of the Third Reich.

So that is the background to the empire. We end up in control of all but one fraction, the eastern fraction of Germany. We put the French in one part; we put the British in another part; we were in a third part. We let Stalin, who was in a rage, only have East Prussia, 'cause we didn't want it; it was without, really, intrinsic value. And we betrayed him. Roosevelt had said Germany will be governed by the four powers together, sharing the same capital, Berlin, and that meant Russia, that meant

France, England, and the United States. Truman with Acheson just reversed that. He did that at Potsdam. So we divided up Germany in sections, and we took all the best parts for ourselves, and then we created a West German republic, which we then started to rearm. Well, Stalin by then was hysterical. Not only had he been cut out of the valuable parts of Germany, but we were rearming Germany. I mean, he just lost twenty million people to the Germans, and here is the United States, whom he thought is his ally, is arming them again, and our blowhards are beginning to talk about international communism is on the march; Stalin is another Hitler, he wants to conquer Europe. I mean, he couldn't conquer anything at this point. Practically, his troops were dead. They'd run out of everything, right down to the boots that the Russians were wearing. They had no idea those boots came from us. They had no clothes left, they had no food, not much ammunition, but they were—they were mad as hell at the Germans. They were going to kill as many Germans as they could, and they did. So Truman gets back to the United States after Potsdam, where he has gotten rid of the Yalta agreements, which Roosevelt had tried to pacify Stalin and make an alliance.

He gets back and the decision is made that we are going to stay armed. We are not going to disarm, 'cause the world is filled with dangerous people like Stalin. So he calls in Congress, the congressional leaders, and he says, "Look, we're going to have to take on Stalin, communism, Russians one of these days, and we'd better be ready for it now. We mustn't disarm." Senator

Vandenberg of Michigan, a Republican whom the Democrat Truman needed, said, "Well, if you want to do that, Mr. President, you're going to have to scare the hell out of the American people, because we—Congress cannot appropriate so much money, particularly in a postwar period where we need everything that we don't have and we must reallocate for peacetime." Truman said, "Don't worry." First thing he did, he—loyalty oaths all throughout the government; everybody had to swear a loyalty oath, throughout the university, throughout high schools, teachers. You've got to go up and swear allegiance to the United States, or else you're a commie. I mean, we had imported fascism.

JAY: Is that when standing up in school and pledging allegiance to the flag come from there?

VIDAL: Well, it was certainly helped by that. I don't know at what instances in the past that that was, you know, a regular thing to do in school, because it never was done in any school I went to, but I had gone to private schools—I think the public schools were obliged to do that. But it was the loyalty oaths that drove former Vice President Henry Wallace, the heir to the New Deal who should have been the president after Roosevelt's death—he went to war against Truman. And he said there was a big crisis going on.

Truman was using a threat that the Russians were going to interfere in the Yugoslav affairs and Greek affairs. And he said—Wallace said, "This is not a Greek crisis as the administration likes to tell us; it's not a Yugoslav crisis; this is an American crisis. We have a government that is now pledging itself and us to fight on the side of any government, no matter how terrible, if it says it's anti-communist or anti-Russian. We're on their side. And we're now demanding of every janitor and every schoolhouse, the United States, to swear loyalty to the Union. We've never done this before. The fact that half the country had been involved in the war, in the military, should have been quite enough to demonstrate the loyalty of the people of the United States. Harry Truman is acting like a European dictator and getting away with it." Why? Because the rulers of the country, just the same as now, corporate America, that makes its money out of armaments and graft and media, thought it was a good idea to frighten the people. The more scared they are, the more they'll appropriate, more tanks you can sell, more—I think we were building B-29s by then—we were long past the B-17. And we were getting ready to go for a hydrogen bomb, having already done an atomic bomb, which to the horror of General Eisenhower and Admiral Nimitz, and even General Curtis LeMay of the air force, Truman went ahead and used it against Japan after the Japanese were—had tried for the better part of a year to surrender. They had no cities left; there was nothing left to knock down. Truman wanted to show the atom bomb worked. He wanted to scare not only Stalin but our allies. And he almost immediately then sent a troop, a fleet of B-29 bombers, I think allegedly with atomic warheads, to the British Isles to protect them from the coming Soviet attack. The Soviet wasn't about to attack England or anybody at that time.

And thus it was, we became totally militarized and what is called a national security state. And the legalisms behind it were national security, document number sixty-eight, I think it was, which—it lists about seven points that would be the constitution of this new state. The Department of War suddenly becomes the Department of Defense. OSS, Office of Strategic Services, which was our spying gang throughout World War II, becomes the CIA. And what has the CIA done, in Europe particularly (it's all over the place)? Well, it makes sure that no liberal or leftist government comes to power. In April 1948, I was in Italy. And this was their first big postwar election. And it was about fifty-fifty between the Communists and the Christian Democrats, and they probably would have split the vote had a coalition government—the Italian communists were no more dangerous, you know, than the vegetarian party ever was in the United States. Italians don't take well to communism: They're too individualistic. But this was another excuse for us to interfere in the election and to make sure that the Christian Democrats have a huge victory. We bought newspapers; we bought magazines. Some of the best literary magazines in Europe were financed by the American government, like *Encounter* in England. I used to write for them, little knowing I was working for the American government. That's what I mean by militarizing: Everything was militarized to fight communism, monolithic, atheistic, and godless (that's much worse than atheistic). Communism forever on the march.

So that changed the United States forever. We have never ceased to be a national security state. We have kept on more and more armaments, year after year, greater and greater appropriations for the military. Once they discover anti-gravity, we have to find out something even further that would deteriorate anti-gravity machines on the ground. So we're in the midst of an arms race which goes on even as you and I sit here to chat. We have been forever at war. Since 1945, people criticize—they often refer to that as the Golden Age; they'd never know what I'm talking about. I try to explain it, and I get tired. The Golden Age was 1945 to 1950. It was only five years. In those five years, in the theater we had *A Streetcar Named Desire*, we had *Death of a Salesman*, we had Lenny Bernstein and music and Aaron Copland. We had a raft of us novelists and poets. The United States, we even had the best ballet in the world, to the horror of the Russians. We had come alive after years of depression and world war. Suddenly the United States was a golden age in culture.

JAY: And in Democratic thought.

VIDAL: There was Democratic thought, and there was Republican thought, and there was liberal thought, and there was conservative thought. Politics was never very big, because we were a culture stirring. Culture is a lot more important than politics, though if you have bad politics, you cannot have good culture, but we didn't know then the roots of the bad politics that were flourishing in our national security state. So I say the

Golden Age was the five years that we were at peace. We had been at war the rest of the time, practically, since the Civil War, Spanish-American War. We were always at war, expansionist, and not a war of the people's seeking.

So the Golden Age starts with the surrender of Japan, the surrender of Germany, and it ends five years later with Korea, in which they hand us our head on the peninsula there, because they misunderstood Dean Acheson, who had made a speech saying we'll fight for this, and we'll fight for, you know, Guatemala, we'll fight for Iran, we'll fight for this, we'll fight for that. And it's a laundry list of where we were in charge and you must obey us. But he left out Korea. And so the North Koreans, being terribly literal, decided, oh, good chance to reunite with South Korea. So they started to march to join up with the southern part of their peninsula. And with that, the Korean War began. We couldn't declare war—this was where we lost the Constitution. Truman did not dare go before Congress, having already got all this money from armaments so that we can have a national security state. So he goes to the United Nations and says, "Can we call it a police action in Korea?" you know, in front of the United Nations. They said, "Well, if that's what you want to do, do that." So we get into a police action. So we either call things police actions or special congressional—and now we have preemptive war: the president arbitrarily can just go over and take a look at—oh, I don't know, at Albania, say, "We don't like your looks," you know, "You could have some terrorists in those hills, so, sorry, we're going to have to blow up Tirana, your capital, because there may be terrorists living there."

JAY: A lot of the wars waged against various people after 1950 are said to be against the Russians, but they're against the Guatemalans, and they're against Africans. What were they afraid of, and how much was this really about what they thought was a Russian threat, and how much was it about national liberation movements?

VIDAL: Well, the trick of the national security state is, first of all, there must always be an enemy, and he's—must be terrifying, and he wants to blow us up because he's evil and we're good. So every day we are brainwashed: The Russians have discovered anti-gravity, or they've done this, or they've done that, and they're evil; we are good, as well as overweight. Things—little things like this matter a great deal in advertising. Great advertising campaign to keep ourselves fully armed to the teeth.

Meanwhile, let me just give you a personal anecdote. I got out of the army in forty-six. I'd written my first novel, and it was published. And Europe wasn't open. Everything had been knocked down. And so I headed south of the border. I wanted to get away and work. If I hung around New York, I wouldn't have done anything. So I went down to—I just kept going south, and I got as far as Guatemala. And I loved a city called Antigua, seventeenth-century city which had been wrecked by earthquakes two or three hundred years ago. So I got a house down there, and I got a seventeenth-century monastery for two thousand dollars, and I settled in, wrote two or three books there.

Meanwhile, I had made some political friends there, one of them being the vice president of the country, who was—I was still in my early twenties, and he was an old man of twenty-seven, but he was vice president. Very smart guy. And they were experimenting. They had a democratically elected government in Guatemala. The president was called Arévalo. He was a philosophy professor who had been teaching in Buenos Aires when Ubico was the American-chosen dictator of Guatemala. This is pre–World War II. And I remember one day sitting in the square in Antigua, and Mario, which was my political friend's name, said, "You know, your government is going to overthrow our government almost anytime." I said, "Come on. We just conquered Japan; we just conquered Germany. What do we want with Guatemala? Nobody knows where it is." And Mario said, "Well, United Fruit knows where it is, and they're the biggest employer in the country. And all of their revenues—which were considerable from selling bananas around the world, which are harvested here—we're trying to tax them just a small amount of money, because we have no money. And your CIA"—which was by then it was brand-new and nobody knew anything about it or that it existed for information— "your CIA is under orders from President Eisenhower to overthrow the government and accuse us of being communist, so that United Fruit will not have to pay tax." Well, we—oh, God, we had rows and rows over this. I said, "Well, the United States doesn't behave like that." You know. I did not know as much history then as I do now. And so it came to pass.

Didn't happen with Arévalo; it happened with the next freely elected president, who was called Jacobo Árbenz. And he wanted to re-create a Roosevelt-style New Deal for Guatemala. And again, free elections. A senator got up—Republican senator—in our Senate and said, "We must do something about Guatemala, because the government is now in the hands of communists, working hand-in-glove with the Soviet Union. And they are about to seize the banana plantations, which are the property of the United Fruit Company." Who was the senator? Henry Cabot Lodge of Massachusetts, who was on the board of directors of United Fruit, and a man I had known all my life as a family friend. And this gracious, patrician New Englander is yelling, "Red! Red! Red! Overthrow them!" At which Eisenhower sent down troops, and they overthrew the government. And after that, it's been one bloodbath after another, military governments, and peace may never be restored there. Some times are better than others. I'm told things are not as bad this year as they were five years ago. That was my first indoctrination in the American Empire in action, and I saw it with my own eyes and heard about it happening. I tried to come back. As I'm a writer, I wrote about these things. Nobody'd publish it. I did do a novel called *Dark Green, Bright Red*, only to have my publishers reluctantly bring it out. And they just shook their heads sadly, and they said, "No, no novel about Latin America has ever sold a copy." Of course, I had predicted Castro, so soon after that a lot of books about that part of the world were published, but by then I was elsewhere.

JAY: You've written that Truman, Eisenhower understood the Cold War as a tactic, but Kennedy was a believer. Talk about this.

VIDAL: Well, the tragedy was, in time, Eisenhower— first he uses the CIA twice, once to overthrow the Guatemalan government, the second time—more dangerously—to overthrow the government of Iran, Prime Minister Mosaddeq, a democratically elected figure, very popular in Iran. Iran is a very sophisticated country. I would say, head-by-head at least, its ruling class is far better educated than ours. So we're almost out of our league when we're taking them on, as we're about to do again. Eisenhower overthrows Mosaddeq, restores the shah, and has already created a permanent bloodbath in Guatemala. Well, along comes Jack Kennedy, and Jack's very bright about many things but he was brought up in the house of a very right-wing man, family, without much imagination about the rest of the world, without much knowledge of the rest of the world. But Jack was a quick learner. But he arrived with all these right-wing views. Well, where Eisenhower and Truman were two old, tough politicians. So Eisenhower had been a soldier all his life, but a soldier-politician knows more about politics than any civilian politician will ever know. Just watch out for a general who has political ambitions. They're very good at it. Neither Truman nor Eisenhower believed in the threat of world communism, but they knew it played for the dum-dums like nobody's business. "Russians are coming. Oh, communists! Godless atheists, godless atheists. Oh, no. Does this mean that we'll have to get up at five o'clock every morning and commit abortions all day long under the Red flag?" "Yes, that's what it means." Oh, this—the dumbest things were pumped into our poor people's heads. And the Russians weren't going anywhere this time. We're still talking about— well, Jack came to power in what, 1960? Khrushchev is trying to make changes. Khrushchev has already made his famous speech denouncing Stalin. He's trying to start a new chapter. Jack, I'm afraid, believed in what the two old presidents knew was cynical nonsense with which they could get elected, and get appropriations for the military, and just have the country on a platter.

Jack was generally high-minded; he wanted to free the world. You know. It was just like Bush, you know, who loves freedom and liberty and so forth and so on. Jack believed it, and that was dangerous. And at one point after sixty-one or sixty-two, I no longer saw him. I could not stand Bobby Kennedy. I stayed away. I wish I had seen him, and I wish I could have talked to him occasionally, because he was a quick study, Mr. Kennedy. And after the Bay of Pigs, when he realized his own advisers were the worst in the world—I mean the CIA telling him that there would be a huge uprising in favor of the United States once they arrived at the Bay of Pigs, not telling him the Bay of Pigs, I think, was permanently underwater or there was something wrong with it. Everything that he was told by Allen

Dulles, who was the head of the CIA then, was untrue.

JAY: The Kennedys in their day, and to a large extent still to this day, were seen as the coming to power of enlightened, out of this sort of narrow Cold War of the fifties. This was now a modern democratic vision, is how it was portrayed.

VIDAL: Well, it has been portrayed after the fact that Jack Kennedy represented, you know, a new generation of Americans born in this century. I often said, "Well, why are you proud of that? The twentieth century is the worst thing the world ever saw." You know. But he liked his rhetoric. He was a new generation. He was attractive, and so was she [Jacqueline Kennedy]. And he was given the benefit of a lot of doubt. He learned as he went along, and he learned not to trust the military experts; he learned a lot of things. I remember his saying to me once, in a period when I was seeing a good deal of him, just before he became president and immediately afterwards he said, "You know, I don't know anybody, just politicians." So he was trying to pick a cabinet. And he'd—he'd go around muttering, "Who the hell is—oh, Dean Rusk. Who is Dean Rusk?" He was haunted by the name, and that of course was going to be his secretary of state. He didn't know who he was. So he was pretty innocent of the people who might have been helpful. He had his playmates, but they were not intellectual folks. There was the occasional Arthur Schlesinger, but Arthur was only at court due to Bobby—it was Bobby who got him into the White House, not Jack. But Jack was very quick and he was—I always thought of him more as a British kid than I did as an American. He knew more British parliamentary history than he knew American history. I mean, he could tell you all about Palmerston, the prime minister. You get him on Andrew Johnson, and he'd blank. But he did read, he did think. He was extremely right wing because his family was. He had no opportunity to be otherwise. Suspicious, however, of intellectuals. And heaven knows people who have a divine wisdom like the Church; he was no friend to the bishops, nor were they any friends to him in his own church. He was feeling his way, but he saw himself in heroic terms. He said once—well, he said it once in my hearing, and certainly, I'm told, to the great link in authority, David Herbert Donald at Harvard, he said, you know, "Where would Lincoln have been without the Civil War? Just another railroad lawyer." You know, that's about it. He figured out wartime presidents, just as this silly little thing we have now as president also goes on and on that he's— "I'm wartime president, wartime president." They know that's how you make it in the history books. They don't seem to realize that is how you can destroy your country, if not physically at least economically by making terrible errors. So it's a very dangerous thing, now, to be a wartime president. The old days, when it's just a few muskets and a gunboat or two, war could be sort of glamorous, but it is not. It seemed to me that he was looking for a war from the very beginning. And there were contingency plans at Eisenhower's White House, with Vice President Nixon in charge of them, to get rid of Castro, and to somehow draw Cuba back into our orbit.

And why and how he fell for it—I'd love to know the discussions that went on; I suppose plenty of them are recorded—when he decided to go ahead, but reluctantly, for what became the Bay of Pigs, a total disaster for the U.S. and for the Cuban émigrés who were in the United States or in Central America being prepared for the invasions. It was just harebrained. He'd also been looking around for the possibilities of a war in Laos. We've always had our eye on Southeast Asia.

JAY: Why?

VIDAL: Wealth. Southeast Asia, plus northeast Asia, which is Manchuria, and Shanxi Province. It was our greatest geopolitical figure, Brooks Adams of the Adams family, who said he who controls Shanxi Province controls the world, because that was the greatest concentration of coal, which was then the fuel, iron ore. It's the richest part. What used to be Manchuria is now North Korea and parts of northern China. All the world had their eye on that. I speak now the end of the nineteenth century, beginning of the twentieth century. Laos was just part of that complex, but further south. Laos didn't play. Jack did make an effort in that direction. Then the domino theory. Eisenhower, who should have known better, seems to have fallen for it. If Cambodia falls, Thailand falls; if Thailand falls, Singapore falls; if Singapore falls—you know, dominoes, dominoes, dominoes. Well, in the real world, great politicians don't play dominoes, they play chess, and we had a bunch of domino players when we should have had a bunch of chess players. They were not smart enough to know how to manipulate all this.

JAY: Take us inside the head of Jack Kennedy. What did he believe in?

VIDAL: Well, what did Jack really believe in? I don't know what he really believed in, and I don't know what anybody really believes in. He was romantic in that he saw himself as a kind of—he knew he was going to die very young. He had been sick all of his life. I mean, the number of things wrong with him. I remember my half sister, who was Jackie's stepsister, describing this when she was about twelve years old: Wherever he was, in whatever household, there was a sickroom, and there were ice boxes with needles; and she remembers opening an ice box—and she'd never seen so much medicine in her life—just to keep him alive. He had Addison's disease—he had no adrenal function. So the clinic thought up a special operation, in which they would put a kind of false adrenal gland under the flesh of the thigh, and they'd put it under there and put some scotch tape over whatever it is to hold it in place, and that would feed him enough adrenaline for a month or so, and have to change it. This was dangerous. This affects your judgment, lack of adrenaline. And then, so many other things were wrong with him. He knew time was short. That's why people wonder why he was so bold in his private life. Well, he wasn't going to live very long. He wanted to have a very good time as quickly as possible, so he did.

And he always said, well, you can't take chances like that. Suppose the press gets onto it. He said, particularly, "When I'm alive," he said, "they don't dare print it." In those days they didn't, particularly if a president is warlike and he was getting more and more warlike. "They won't print it. And when I'm dead, I don't care." So he had it covered. I would think he was a guy who enjoyed life, who didn't expect to live very long, who wanted to make his mark, believed in the Cold War, or he believed in the White Knight versus the Wicked Knight, and he was going to be the White Knight, and he was going to win. So I think he was more tolerant of the idea of war.

The missile crisis really scared him. Also, I remember talking to him when he came back from the Vienna conference with Khrushchev, and I was full of the usual liberal complaints, and I said, "But, you know, there seems to be so really little at issue between our side and their side." I said, "It's pretty clear Khrushchev isn't marching anywhere," and Jack quite agreed to that, even though he had to pretend how dangerous the Soviet Union was, and they're getting ahead of us in firecrackers and popcorn and this and that, that he had to do all that rhetoric. He said, "No." But he said—he had one line which was very interesting about these things. They said something about, well, actually, what Khrushchev has done here and there, and I think it was apropos, putting the missiles in Cuba, did they really change? And, of course, you know, we didn't know they had atomic weapons, heads to them. And somebody said, "Well, what does that do to the balance of power?

It doesn't change anything. United States is a huge country; that's a little island down there. So they might knock out some cities, and that might be very unpleasant for the people knocked out, but we're not going to be defeated by some Russian missiles." And he said, "No." But he said, "In this kind of politics, it is the appearance of things that matters." So in the long run, we go back to my notion that the only art form the United States has ever created is the TV commercial. That is our art form, and that's how we control people. Which is a normal response to somebody who was a creation of advertisers, as was Eisenhower, as was everybody else, as was Khrushchev. And it's a world of illusions, and it's a world of false claims. And I think Jack made the joke once—Khrushchev made the joke to Jack at Vienna. They were talking about Eisenhower and the spy plane, which had been such an embarrassment to the previous administration, and Khrushchev had made a joke at the time. He said, "I wanted to propose to the president of the United States that we'd both save a lot of money if we hired the same people and paid for them as spies, 'cause they come to both sides, anyway. So we'd just save, each of us, 50 percent of what we now spend on spying." And the Americans gave pretty sick laughs to that, but Khrushchev got the point to that.

JAY: Everything being illusion, and the extent to which these political figures were acting out a theater, the media wasn't any better then, either. And how much did that have to do with the intimidation that came out of McCarthyism?

VIDAL: Well, everything is knotted together. Harry Truman, with the loyalty oaths and terrifying everybody that there was a communist under every bed and every schoolhouse, made it possible for Senator McCarthy to conduct a career of terror, accusing this one and that one of communism. And you'd think his fellow senators would have known how to put him in a box, but they didn't know how, and he was allowed to go on much, much, much too long. And Eisenhower was no strongman during all this. Eisenhower, however, was a very shrewd politician. He just knew let this guy rave on and he'll hang himself. He raved on, and he hung himself. Not to say that Eisenhower wasn't there, you know, opening the trapdoor so McCarthy fell through and strangled.

JAY: But he also played a useful role for them.

VIDAL: Well, he got out the vote of hot-eyed Republicans.

JAY: And cleaned out much of the press and much of Hollywood.

VIDAL: Well, they didn't clean out. It was meant, of course, to intimidate Hollywood and the media. Well, the media already belongs to the McCarthyite people, much of it, and Hollywood is always craven and easily influenced—blacklists can do it every time. When I was writing plays for live television back in the fifties, there was a guy—we called him the Butcher of Schenectady, I think it was—guy with a big grocery store. That was all. He decided who was a communist across the country. And he'd be told that Zsa Zsa Gabor was a communist. So any program she was on, any advertiser, Zsa Zsa Gabor (I'm just making up the name—I don't know), he would refuse to sell the products of anybody who paid for a program she appeared on. That's how the blacklist started.

Now, the Butcher of Schenectady would also say you could clear yourself if you came to Schenectady on your knees, and he'd give you absolution if you swore never to do it again. So a lot of very famous stars went up to Schenectady to see this guy. And that was very much in control for quite a few years.

I was a playwright, so I was able to pick my cast in those days. It was not a director's medium; it was a writer's meeting. And I'd say—I remember I'd say I wanted Gale Sondergaard for something. She was a wonderful actress. And I told the producer—I said, "Are we getting Sondergaard?" And he said, "Fourteenth floor." That was the floor where the censorship was done. Never said anything more than that, she's blacklisted, you can't use her.

JAY: So when Kennedy emerges, there's already a culture in the news media that, if you take your critique past a certain line, you might be called a communist. Is there a kind of self-censorship that emerges throughout this whole next decade?

VIDAL: Oh, I think it still exists, only it isn't

communism anymore, it's terrorism: You're supporting terrorism, and you're not supporting our brave guys and gals; you're not a patriot. I'm surprised—if we had a decent media, which we do not have or anything close, these people wouldn't be allowed to get away with this stuff. They'd just be stopped. Who's interested in what the Butcher of Schenectady has to say on any subject? He doesn't know anything. So he boycotts an actress. Raise a legal defense fund and sue him. You know, that's the normal American way. It still goes on, but it's so weak.

I did a little book called *Perpetual War for Perpetual Peace*, and I tried to explain what the motives of an Osama bin Laden were for hitting us. Couldn't say that he's evil. He does it for kicks. And, I said, presumably we never did anything to upset him and the Muslims and Saudi Arabia. No. How could we? We're the good people. And then you realize, and you look into these vacant American newscaster eyes, that you've got a bunch of real maniacs or terrified maniacs, which is rather worse, so they get away with it.

JAY: How we got into that segue was, why did Kennedy buy this thing about Cuba, appearance, because he's a man of creative appearance himself. So let's get back to Kennedy, Cuba, Bay of Pigs.

VIDAL: Well, I think Kennedy had it in mind when he got to be president, you know, his inaugural address gives it away: "We'll bear any burden, to see that liberty"—whatever it was—"triumphs around the world." Well, you know, I muttered to myself, "You do it alone, Jack. I'm not going to help you bearing any burden." I said, "The only time that the Soviet Union would begin to bother me as a threat to America would be when the Russians figure out how to get a proper screw-on lid to the vodka bottle." They were still struggling in 1960. In the 1970s, they'd got something—it was like tinfoil. You know, you'd like this, and then suddenly you'd have this flat thing in your hand. I said, "One day, they'll get it. And probably they'll blow us up one night. I'm just waiting until that decent cap to the vodka bottle has been invented by these maniacs driven by malice and rage."

They were no competition for us, and we knew it, and they knew that we knew it. But they had to make certain noises for their people; we had to make certain noises for our people. The arms race was just as good for their rich people as it was for our rich people, and that's why we had the arms race. [As for] Jack, I think—I think the Bay of Pigs waked him up—I mean the missile crisis. I think the missile crisis woke him up when he saw how easily the world could end.

JAY: One version of the events is that he was actually ready to fire and had to be talked out of firing weapons.

VIDAL: I don't think I've heard rumors that he was very much in favor of it, of blowing up the missile sites on Cuba.

JAY: No, no, no. The story I've heard from fairly

credible people was he was ready to actually fire a first-strike on the—that he thought the Russians might strike. During the Cuban missile crisis, the time Khrushchev had said he wouldn't back down, that Jack actually took the position that he's getting ready to fire on us and we should fire, and that actually the military talked him out of firing.

VIDAL: Yeah. It was almost the opposite. They were talking about everything during the missile crisis. And Washington being Washington, you hear everything that they were talking about sooner or later. And Jack held to the line. After all, he'd been encouraged into the Bay of Pigs by the military, by military intelligence. He's not about to take them seriously, but they were advising him to go ahead and take out those missiles, not knowing until long after, when they held the meetings down there in Cuba, did we find out that they had nuclear warheads, and we would have blown up a lot of the island, and they could hit us as far north as Seattle. We would lose every city from Seattle down to Miami. That was known at the White House. Well, it was not known that they had the weapons, but they know that they had the range.

At no point was he the hawk. He made hawkish noises where it seemed—after all, appearance, appearance—you've got to seem to be ready to go. So he was at times very ready to go. I can remember I went up to Hyannis Port to see Jack and Jackie. This was August 1961. This is when the Berlin Wall was going up. And curiously enough, Jackie, who was pretty apolitical, was in a rage over it, and she said, "I just—I don't understand what's going on." And I said, "Well, it's pretty clear that the Russians are making trouble for us in Berlin." I didn't say anything about the fact that I also felt we'd made so much trouble for them by dividing up Germany and by giving them the lousy eastern end and making such a fuss over Berlin itself. He had to do something, Khrushchev. And as we look back, building a wall was not the world's worst thing; it was a great propaganda coup for us. But I remember it was, we were sitting there in his living room in the Kennedy Compound at Hyannis Port. It was a very spare room. And Jack is puffing on his cigar and reading through—he'd just got a letter from de Gaulle, and he was testing his French to see how good it was (it was awful). But he was trying to read it in French. And Jackie was carrying on. And she said—looking at Jack, and theoretically, at all the other people around, in the nearby houses within the compound, she said, "To think that they could let something go this far"—'cause, you know, she had to believe the press too, and the press was hysterical. "And taking into account, you know, all the children that are going to be killed. Don't they take anything into account?" I mean, she had finally faced war. Up until now, I mean, she'd had no great decisions in her life, aside from aesthetic ones.

They really meant this thing, because they were talking war, Jack was talking war. And he'd got a desperate letter, which I finally did read—not then, but later when it was published—from de Gaulle that said, "Under no circumstances go back and talk to

Khrushchev. The last time you did was a disaster. He thought you were weak, and he's made trouble for you ever since. Don't do it." And Jack didn't. So to be there at that time—I made notes too. It's in my memoir, *Palimpsest*. I took about fourteen pages of notes, everything that was said amongst us and two or three people who came by for dinner and so on. And it was only Jackie who was really in a rage over all this. And her attitude really was, you know, men are such a mess. I mean, she suddenly was going back to the ancient Greeks, you know, and they're going to boycott the men if they're going to try to kill everybody.

JAY: What happens to the development of the national security state under Kennedy?

VIDAL: National security state under Kennedy blossomed, of course. After all, he ordered, after the Berlin Wall, the biggest buildup in our history until then. I think just sort of bullet by bullet it was larger than the one Roosevelt had ordered in 1940. Not as effective, but it was a pretty big one, and the largest one in peacetime. Roosevelt could at least argue war is at hand. So the national security state was doing very well. Jack I don't think really understood it, and what he did understand, he didn't much care about it. He was— he was not a true believer. And remember it is a nation full of hot-eyed maniacs, as we see every now and then at election times. And fluorine in the water was a great issue when Jack was president, you know, and he was suspected of—he and the pope would go out every evening and put fluorine in the water to help people's teeth from rotting away, and that was evil.

JAY: It must have worked. You said those guys had good teeth—and their children—at that period.

VIDAL: Yeah, absolutely. Well served by the Cold War and the national security state.

JAY: Bobby Kennedy and his role in all of it.

VIDAL: Obscure.

Well, Bobby Kennedy, during the missile crisis, as far as we know, gave very good counsel, and he was the one who was dealing with the Russian ambassador regularly and keeping him up to date on what they were doing. So Bobby was sort of the link to the Kremlin through Ambassador—I forget his name. So he was a useful citizen. And then the thought of him as a liberal president representing the New Deal was something that's just nonsense. He's a virulent right winger. After all, he was a great buddy of Senator McCarthy. He was on McCarthy's committee, along with Roy Cohn, and they were both sort of great friends of Joe McCarthy. He was rather insensitive to those things until he becomes the heir and Jack is dead, and then he begins to wrap himself in the mantle of Franklin Roosevelt.

JAY: So Jack is assassinated. Do we know by whom?

VIDAL: Well, Jack was killed, I assume, by the Mafia.

I've never heard an explanation which made more sense than that. It was due to his father's connection as a leading bootlegger, that is, somebody importing, illegally, alcohol during the period of Prohibition in the 1920s in the United States. And his father's right-hand man was Frank Costello from the New York mob.

JAY: Kennedy and a certain trend within the Democratic Party had this hate-on for Castro, which continues to this day. But why such a profound hate for Castro?

VIDAL: Well, Kennedy's hatred for Castro was Castro didn't throw up his hands and cry uncle. Castro fought him to his knees: Bay of Pigs was an extraordinary blow to a new president, and Jack didn't think he'd ever get over it. And that's why he started to send troops into Vietnam. He told old Albert Gore, father of the recent vice president—and old Albert was a senator from Tennessee. And he saw him just before he went to Dallas to be assassinated. And everybody was concerned. You know, what are you going to do? Because Castro was making menacing noises and so on. And to the pacifists, Jack was saying, oh, he'd have the troops back. The elections—it's 1963. The election's next year, 1964. By November 1964 most of them will be home. And he meant rotation: He didn't mean he was going to withdraw them; they'd just be rotated back and others would be sent out.

He had sent out—just to show how tough he was, after the Bay of Pigs, it was necessary to win a war somewhere or appear to be dominant militarily somewhere. He came to the conclusion that French Indochina, which had been greatly helped—Roosevelt wanted the French out; Truman was persuaded to leave the French in. The French stayed in, and they got their heads handed to them by the Vietcong. Then Eisenhower was secretly helping the French, which he should not have been doing. Jack is in a funny situation, because Jack was anti-French policy when he was in the Senate, particularly over Algiers. He thought the French should get out of Algiers. So Jack was rather anti-colonial. But now he has looked weak after the Bay of Pigs. He's got to do something dominant. There is Indochina. Vietcong is doing terribly well up there in the north, so he sends advisers over. Twenty thousand, I think, was the first shipment, all armed, and all partaking in the defense of the imperial family in Saigon, which was—it was all Catholic, by the way, and all friends of Joe Kennedy. And Madame Mary knew how these names come back. So he sends these troops over. Is there to be a buildup? Are we really going to go to war, then? To most of the doves he was saying, "No, no, no, it's just showing the flag; we've got to get ready for the next election, got to look strong, appearances, appearances, got to look strong in Indochina." Old Albert Gore asked him, well, just before he left for Dallas, "Well, what are your intentions?" 'Cause he seemed to be building up down there. And he says, "After the Bay of Pigs, I've got to go all the way with this one. And he said the same thing—and I was told this by the editor of the *Christian Science Monitor*, whose name I can no longer remember—he had told him the same thing. Take your pick. He certainly wouldn't have stayed on year after year after year after year, as he was not stupid, as Nixon proved to be and as Johnson proved to be—they stayed too long at the fair. But he certainly was gung ho for war, and yes, he tried to kill Castro a number of times. Operation Mongoose it was called. He was a thwarted rich boy. "How dare you beat me at my own game in my own backyard?"

JAY: So by the death of Kennedy, where are we at in terms of the maturation of the convergence of the intelligence apparatus, the CIA, arms producers, the Pentagon, politicians?

VIDAL: Well, today we're in a peculiar limbo, and since 9/11 things that have never happened to us before have started to happen. Nine/eleven, whoever is behind it—I assume it's Osama bin Laden and some Muslim fanatics—but whoever's behind it is not important, as you can tell. We haven't tried to find him, for one thing. If he were important, we would. So it means our own government doesn't—doesn't much care. But 9/11 proved to be a pretext for getting rid of the old republic, which has not been in very good shape for a long, long time, starting with the national security state, which made us a totally militarized society—that's Harry Truman. And ever since, we just go further and further along the road toward total war for nearly everybody. Now we're in a strange, strange situation. There is nothing in our history to guide us; we've never been in this situation in which one gang basically has seized power. We've been very lucky: never—we've had dictators before. Lincoln was a dictator, but he was a dictator of the republic. The republic still stood when he was dictator, and we needed him. Franklin Roosevelt was a dictator, and we needed him. And they were—only briefly were they dictators. Now we have a dictatorial system, as best personified by the USA Patriot Act, which just removes us of our Bill of Rights. This is the most serious thing that has happened in the history of the United States, and how we get out of it's anyone's guess.

JAY: If Kennedy goes into Vietnam to prove strength after the weakness of Cuba, Vietnam ends up a more profound show of weakness than even Cuba. How does that color what happens from 9/11 on?

VIDAL: I don't think that you can use Kennedy and Vietnam. After all, Vietnam was lost—if we ever had it—by the likes of Nixon and Lyndon Johnson. Kennedy's dead by then. Yes, Kennedy went in there, but we don't know—

JAY: I don't mean Kennedy. In terms of the need of the empire to have the appearance of strength, there's a need to somehow overcome this defeat in Vietnam, is there not?

VIDAL: It could be argued that the defeat in Vietnam, in the minds of some hawks, could be undone by standing tall in the oil fields of the Middle East. But other forces are at work. There is no doubt that we stand tall in the eyes of the world, because we have the power to kill everyone on earth. Everybody knows it.

And I think the more they watch these loons that have taken charge of our government, the more they fear perhaps something like this could happen, that we might get an administration that was going to try to blow up North Korea. And then, while they're at it, "Oh, let's take out Beijing too. They've been such a nuisance, you know." We have very ignorant people governing the country, and they're full of hate for everybody, including the American people. We are the real enemies of the current rulers.

No. What I see is we're all dressed up and nowhere to go, logically speaking. The so-called neoconservatives are given lots of credit for our current bellicosity and all the wars that we seem to be ready to fight. They got us into Iraq, which—we had no reason to attack Iraq. We looked tall there. The president's father went into Panama, and when they asked, "Why did you go in there? That's a nothing little country. Why did you go in there and knock it down?" And one of old President Bush's advisers said, "Well, we did it because we could do it. Like Grenada, we could do it." In other words, it's good for people, for us, to show our strength every now and then, and that we're not afraid of killing people. In fact, we kind of like it.

Well, we're getting a very bad rep. Now we are poised. The world is running out of fossil fuel. Instead of working morning, noon, and night trying to find replacements for it, whether it's hydrogen or whatever, we're getting ready to seize more oil fields. We've got our eye on Iran, we have the fields in Iraq, we have our eye on Caspian oil, the pipelines that run through Afghanistan down through Pakistan to Karachi, which is where we were headed originally before the Taliban imploded on us. That's what we were going to do. With the pipeline we were going to ship oil down from central Asia, all those countries that end in –*stan*. We were going to send it down to Karachi and put them aboard ships for China. China, I noticed, and the people building that pipeline that we went to war in Afghanistan to get hold of it again, the owners of it are Unical, a California oil firm, which as of this morning's newspaper, China has just bought. Yes, the world is getting smaller, and we're getting a little bit more tight, due to the shrinkage of the world and the rise of China. So we are facing bad times. Now we have fallen into the hands of a group that calls itself neoconservative. You can argue that some of them are acting as super-Zionists, because they think what they're doing is going to be good for Israel. It isn't, but that's one excuse to be used. Others say it's just going to be good for America to be in control of all the oil fields that we can get our hands on, because then we can blackmail everybody, and we are the only people that have the oil.

I understand theft, I think every American understands theft, and a case can be made for it. How was any empire ever developed without theft? So my eyes do not fill with tears when I think of that. But when I think of religious wars, taking on a billion Muslims, exacerbating the Muslim-Jewish wars, and Palestine. There's a lot of places where there's a lot of trouble and a lot of suicide bombers. So we're sort of like somebody going along—I don't know—in a mine field, you know, dropping matches, just dropping matches, waiting— waiting to hear the bang. Well, the bang might take us all out. So as we have chatted our way through much of American history in the course of this conversation, I think everybody should take a sober look at the world about us, remember that practically everything that you're told about other countries is untrue; what we're told about ourselves and our great strength and how much loved we are, forget it. Our strength is there, but it's the kind of strength that blows off your hand while you hold up the grenade; it's a suicidal strength as well as a murderous one. So here we are, and let us hope it is not the end of the road, even though there's every sign that it is not the yellow brick road up ahead.

JAY: I'm just going to ask for one short piece I can use in a different context. Why do you think we need this network? Why do we need The Real News Network?

VIDAL: Well, I think we need now, and we have needed for decades, an honest network news system.

I think it's pretty clear as we look about us, turn on the TV, with the richness that is offered us by cable, by network, by this, by that, that here we are with all these forms of information, and really very ignorant of what's going on in the world. We're not told, or we're given such a distorted view, that even if we were asked to make up our minds—and they don't do that at election time; they just tell us what to think. We need an alternative to advertising. That's all we get. We're nothing but a consumer society with TV manufactured to get us to be loyal consumers and docile workers. Well, we've got to do better than that, because our lives depend on information. Knowledge is power. With no knowledge we'll all die. So it's time, somehow, through the magic of the airwaves, we become informed, because if we aren't, we won't be here to be informed.

GORE VIDAL AT THE REAL NEWS FUNDRAISER
LOS ANGELES 2005

VIDAL: You know, in 1776—I've been tagged as a historian, so I may as well strike a boring note or two. Seventeen seventy-six, when the British occupied Boston, New York City, we were having a revolution. General Washington was our commanding general. The troops kept disappearing at regular intervals.

What was our first move? To free ourselves and get— "I'm a wartime president." What the wartime president says is: Independence is what everybody wants, liberty, freedom. So what was our first move? We invaded Canada. The British were sitting in Boston, sitting in New York. We've lost everything in sight. We wanted Canada right off.

The War of 1812 did not go very well for us. They set fire to the White House, the British, the Capitol. In charge was Admiral Cockburn, whose descendant writes for the *Nation*. You've probably all read Alex. He's perfectly capable of setting fire to all of this again. So that was our second invasion of Canada.

Nowadays, everybody apologizes. You know, I apologize to Samoans that we may have been rude to over the years. I'm happy to apologize to Canada and welcome the counter invasion. You may save us from ourselves.

Now, I'm a C-SPAN junkie. I was brought up in Washington, DC, in the house of a senator, and I'm afraid that I am addicted to boredom. There's no hearing so boring that I do not find it orgasmic. I even listen to the agriculture. Yes, I do. And I remember my grandfather, who was chairman of that committee—I forget what he had done to get to that stage, but he was chairman of agriculture. And the guy who ran the Grange, which is like a collective for farmers across the country, would always begin by addressing the committee by saying, "Senator, for the last twenty years, the crops have been below average." My grandfather would roar with laughter, and the Grange never knew what he was laughing at—the absence of norms, of course.

Now, I have been sort of working with Mr. Conyers. I've never met him, but I'm just a fan. He went out to Ohio with several other members of Congress and some dedicated staffers, and they went from county to county, electoral district to electoral district, and they collected a great deal of material, all of which is purest dynamite, on how that election was stolen and collusion between high officials, like the secretary of state of the state of Ohio, who is in charge of elections, and his hand is in everything.

It was a marvelous and brave thing that Conyers and his fellows from the House of Representatives, from the minority, did. I'm sure you've been reading about it in the press. I wrote a preface, and I said, well, put it on the cover, since my little books sometimes do well out there in the dark. This is not vanity. Just put it on, just so you'll get some space in the bookstore. Oh, they said, this is the report. I said, yes, but there are great interests that don't want anyone to know what happened in Ohio. It proved to be the case. Where is the newspaper of record, that great newspaper, which is always on the wrong side when it has determined which side it ought to be on. There's no review of this book. It's the only explanation of what happened in Ohio.

I was on Bill Maher the other night, and the party line, Democratic Party line was, "Oh, Gore, why go into that? The election's over, so they got it again." I said, "But they didn't get it again. They stole it again." Now, if they steal two in a row and they've got four years to 2008, my God, you're going to see stealth on such a scale as never seen before. And we're not to bother about it because nobody likes sour grapes. You know that. You're supposed to bow.

Well, I learned a great lesson. I have done something like twenty or thirty call-ins around the country. Luckily, they're early in the morning, which is not my hour by any means, but I stay in bed. And suddenly, at seven o'clock, "Mr. Vidal, this is Dallas calling. You're on the air." And I say, "Yes, wonderful, wonderful to be back here in Dallas. How's the weather there?" I'm trying to wake up during all this. I've done at least thirty cities, and we talk about nothing. I haven't had one bad caller. Everybody wants to know what happened in Ohio and how they can get the book. Well, the book is in the bookstores. It's a cheap paperback that was put out by a firm in Chicago. And yet they cannot get a single print interview in the United States of America on a subject of more interest to us than anything else the *New York Times* can find to publish: Who stole the election? Sometimes reminding us who stole it before.

That is the value of what our Canadian friends have come up with. This is kind of a last chance. People say, oh, it can't work. Well, nothing can work till it does. And of course it can.

We are starved for news. Big news. I got a call from Europe a week or two ago. Biggest news all over Europe, headlines. The genius who knocked down all those cities in Iraq and Afghanistan, Rumsfeld, was up in front of an audience in Norway. Now, Norwegians are very polite people. They booed him down, and he couldn't finish his speech. It was all over the European press, and not one word in the American press. And there were some wonderful pictures of Rumsfeld fleeing before crazed Norsemen. So not even for a good picture will they break the silence.

And that brings to mind a favorite quotation of mine, which I always get wrong. Sixteenth century. Montaigne wrote, "Of all the crimes, human crimes, telling lies is the worst and should be a capital offense. Once the tongue gets into the habit of lying, it cannot stop." We now live in a period in which everything we hear is a lie. And we can't necessarily blame the low level of people in our politics, though that's part of it. I think much more serious is the only art form that the United States has created in our two-hundred-odd years, our only art form has been the television commercial. We haven't done well at the other arts.

Saul Bellow's ghost is now looking down on me with a grinding of teeth. But anyway, we haven't done very well at the others. But getting people on television to buy things that they do not need or are bad for them, that has been a superb art. Then when we transfer to selling detergents to selling presidents, lying came into its own.

Then, when they discovered the simple law which every child used to, of my generation, learn—"Rinso White, Rinso White, Rinso White"—repetition. Saddam Hussein, 9/11, Osama bin Laden, Osama bin Laden, 9/11, over and over and over again. Seventy percent of our people now think Osama bin Laden and Saddam Hussein were working together to blow us up, when both men hated each other and had nothing to do with each other.

You rather despair, because he who tries to tell the truth is called the biggest liar of all. Machiavelli, that kindly old cynic, came up with some wonderful advice in *The Prince*, which has been taken seriously by—Karl Roverino, I believe, is probably his correct name. Mr. Rove and company have taken up the fact that the bigger the lie, the more apt it is to be believed. So they're always stretching it, kind of: "You don't think that'll work? My God, it did." Then they go out and take polls, and things are working. Machiavelli—I was reminded of it.

The only thing that Kerry had going for him was that he was an authentic war hero in the adventures in Vietnam. And one of the principal things that W. has going against him is that he is the yellow rose of Texas.

So how do you balance that out? You pay a bunch of guys to come out and say, "Kerry was a coward. He didn't earn those Purple Hearts. He didn't earn that Silver Star. It's all fake. He lied. He lied. He lied." Well, repeat that a thousand times, and we have enough dum-dums in the country, you know, to more than fill a balloting place. And they did. And I thought, my God, these old, simple rules from the fourteenth, fifteenth, sixteenth century are hot as ever in the hands of totally unscrupulous gas and oil people. And that's what we got in charge of us. And we do not turn to them for truth.

JAY: There's a quote from Dan Rather where he said, "I give the White House the benefit of the doubt, whether it's Republican or Democrat." I think we need a television news network that does *not* give the White House the benefit of the doubt, Republican or Democrat.

So independent journalism to us means independent economics. And the core of that, why we think it's possible, is the Internet. We think the web has democratizing potential, and we think this network will be a way to realize much of that potential. It's a convergence of a marriage of citizen journalism with professional journalism. It's a marriage of the web with conventional television, where we're going to use the web to drive viewership to TV. And it's the power of the web to raise money directly from people.

So if our hypothesis is correct that there are millions of people like the people in this room that feel a sense of urgency about this, then it will work. And we launched our website a couple of days ago, and we wanted a soft launch. We didn't make any noise about it. But one—the *Daily Kos* got hold of a Canadian article about us, and there's now be 932 blog reports in the last three days. We're up about—I think we've hit twenty thousand visits in the last three days, and two hundred individual donors, when we really haven't even started asking for money on the web yet. So either we've hit the only two hundred people in the United States that want to give us money, or we're onto something.

Please ask questions of either of us.

AUDIENCE MEMBER: A question for Mr. Vidal. You mentioned the oil oligarchy. And I'm curious if you ever asked yourself, what do these people really want? Are they trying to create a little feudal state for themselves and the rest of us be damned?

VIDAL: What about—I'll repeat your question. The oil oligarchy, oil-igarchy, which governs us at the moment, it's always had great power in the land.

What do they really want? Well, oil to one side, they want power. And there was a famous meeting, which we're still trying to find out—Congress is still trying to find out who was at it—which was called by Vice President Cheney when he first barged into office. And he called in a number of experts, geologists and CEOs.

Everything leaks in Washington, so we know fairly well the sort of people who were there, certainly what they were talking about, quite sensibly. Cheney is not an idiot. He just has a character problem.

But the first question you would ask is: When is the world going to run out of oil at the rate it's being used today? Smart of him to ask it, you know? I can't imagine Kerry remembering to ask it. You know, he'd be too busy, perhaps, explaining something else.

So the report was, that I got, that went around Washington, it was something like—it was pretty dire. It was something like by 2020 we would really be at a danger point in the world supply of fossil fuels, so something must be done. Well, since then we've declared war on two countries that were innocent of any desire to harm us, and one of them has the second greatest oil reserves in the world. Then we find ourselves making a grab for Caspian oil and the famous pipeline that the Taliban were supposed to protect but they didn't. So we had to get rid of the Taliban. And it runs through Afghanistan and it goes down into Pakistan to Karachi, where the oil was all set to be put on board ships. And we'd already made a deal to sell that oil to China.

They do look ahead, these people. You've got to say that for them. But not for our benefit. So I would say it was just naked economic greed and a genuine sense of necessity.

However, since they seem collectively to lack any mind at all, instead of putting the money that they put into—for the fun of knocking down foreign countries, they should have put it in looking for other forms of fuel. I mean, hydrogen has possibilities. Soybeans are finally having their day in the sun. [*applause*]

JAY: Soybeans get applause.

VIDAL: Well, the soybean—who wouldn't applaud the soybean? You know? They've had such trouble.

And so that's really what it's about.

Now we're aiming at Iran. The rumors in Washington (true or false we'll soon know): around August we'll be heading toward Iran from bases which are being established in eastern Afghanistan. That'll be our next war.

What nobody takes into account, since these people are as ignorant as any group that has ever governed the United States—I mean, these people are not to be believed—they don't know that Persia is one of the oldest and greatest cultures in the history of the Earth. They're sitting on a sea of oil. They have worked out uranium deposits. They've worked out nuclear weapons. And if you get them grumpy, they're going to drop them on us, and we the people are going to be killed, because they, the gas and oil lobby, will have their islands off Samoa. They'll be taking trips when the bad days come, or maybe, dare I say it, they will be enjoying the rapture. But, then, I'm an optimist.

AUDIENCE MEMBER: I have a question. It's more of a historical question. And I wondered if you had the answer to it. Outside of what I've read about the Kennedy election—outside of that election, that I'm aware of, and the elections, obviously, with the Bush administration, do you know historically of any other administration that has so blatantly stolen an election historically at this point?

VIDAL: Has the stealing of elections gone on before? I'm afraid it's an old American tradition. I hate to say that, because it gives the enemy all kinds of weapons. You see, Franklin Roosevelt did it, but he at least was funny about it. Eleanor Roosevelt was my neighbor up on the Hudson, and I got to know her very well. And she was very candid and very—a brilliant politician. And she said, "You know, my Franklin was running for the state senate in Dutchess County." This is 1910. "I came to him, and I said, 'Franklin, do you realize that right here in Dutchess County, people are buying votes?' And my Franklin said, 'Don't worry, dear, the Republicans are buying them too.'"

16265841R00083

Printed in Poland
by Amazon Fulfillment
Poland Sp. z o.o., Wrocław